THE RETIREMENT APPROACH FREE OF TAX STRATEGY

HOW TO BUILD YOUR TAX-FREE NEST EGG... WITHOUT RISK!

LAURETT ELLSWORTH ARENZ

Dedicated

To the Man

I have witnessed reinvent himself in several different

industries, including in our marriage!

The Man who I adored enough to marry twice;

He is the love of my life:

David Arenz

Thank you for being my mentor, my business partner,

my husband and best friend.

Making it into our retirement years together

has magnified the good times,

and made every bit of struggle worth it.

Thank you for your continual support and love.

Your Wife

Table of Contents

Contents vii

Foreword ix

Preface... xi

Acknowledgements xiii

Just so YOU know xv

Chapter 1: Your Nest Egg 17

Chapter 2: Triple Crown of Sound Investing 31

Chapter 3: Eliminating the Risks 43

Chapter 4: Tax-Deferred vs. Tax-Free 55

Chapter 5: The Retirement Approach Free of Tax (RAFT) 72

Chapter 6: The Living Benefits of the RAFT in Action 86

Chapter 7: The Personal Pension Plan (PPP) Program 105

Chapter 8: Planning Your Future with the PPP 120

Chapter 9: The Asset Accumulation Access (AAA) Approach....131

Chapter 10: The Triple Crown Solution at Work 142

Epilogue 151

Glossary 153

Resources 169

About the Cover 171

Foreword

Throughout the years I have held many business leadership positions in three different industries. I have trained thousands of managers, salespersons, and financial advisers. I admit that I've not always been the easiest person with whom to work, as I set high standards for myself and for those I train. As a result, many filter away, but those who stay are grateful that they have been thrown into the 'refiner's fire'. These individuals can truly say they are better off intellectually and financially because of the extra effort they exerted. They, in turn, continue to set high standard for themselves and others.

I mentioned the work ethic because I believe it transfers to one's desire to seek and learn the most updated information. When I look at applying new concepts, I evaluate how it pertains to me and my family and I weigh the pros and cons of every detail. When I discovered the strategies described in this book, I was very critical because sometimes the solutions and programs almost seemed to be too good to be true. Yet, as I examined the features, benefits and even the restrictions of the RAFT Strategy, the PPP Program and the AAA Approach, I realized they were solid as a rock. I soon developed relationships with strong companies to offer sound financial solutions during these unpredictable years of Market volatility, rising taxes and impending inflation. Today I am proud to report that we have been able to help thousands escape a potential retirement catastrophe.

Because Laurett loves people, and truly wants to help them achieve a life of abundant prosperity, she has poured her heart and soul into presenting these life-changing ideas in a way that the reader can relate to, remember, and apply. As you are read this book, keep in mind the strategies are not for everyone; your situation is unique. Because of your age, health, and current financial stability, you may or may not be suited to apply every Jewel of the Triple Crown Solution. Until you understand what these concepts are and how they work, you won't know how they might apply to you. I highly encourage you to review these pages with a mind to finding solutions for yourself and your family because this may be your opportunity to take charge of your financial future.

David Arenz

Preface

I t all started in back in 1997 when I was crowned Mrs. Virginia and went on to win my first national pageant title. Because of the Title and experience, I was honored to be promoted by the National Speakers Association. That year I developed a series of seminars entitled HERO'S Strategies for Success, which I presented throughout the country to businesses, government agencies, church groups, and in individual coaching sessions.

HERO'S is an acronym for Health, Education, Relationships, Opportunities, and Spirituality. As a Life Coach, I help individuals create balance in all areas of their life; Physical, Mental, Social, Financial, and Spiritual. I have empowered others in the areas of fitness, cognitive skills development, personality profiling, and I have even taught Seminary. Still, the one piece of the HERO'S coaching I wanted to develop was assisting my clients with their financial future through retirement planning.

At the time, my husband, Dave, owned a mortgage company. He would come home at night after meeting with clients all day, and discuss his cases with me. He shared with me that the homeowners with whom he worked often expressed that they wanted to separate the equity from their homes and invest it, in order to make a greater return. As he searched for the best ways to help his clients, he came across a method of investing home equity into financial instruments that historically gave an 8-9% average tax-free rate of return. This idea gave rise to another meaning of HERO'S (Home Equity Retirement Optimal Solutions), which we ultimately came to use when explaining home equity harvesting.

As my husband and I continued exploring ways to help our mortgage clients succeed financially, we came across the little known, yet extremely powerful strategies we talk about on HERO'S Talk Radio: Freedom Financial Network. These solutions are provided by strong, solvent insurance companies that have been in business for many decades, and some for more than a century. This incredible 16 year journey has totally turned my life around and afforded me the opportunity to help thousand succeed in all areas of their lives. As Dave and I explored resources to offer on our radio program, we came across several books that showcased some of the strategies we endorse. Yet, none contained the full Triple Crown Solution that we speak of over the radio waves. I realized it was my responsibility to *write the right* and *craft the RAFT.*

Between running two businesses, a radio program, and an insurance agency, attending to the children and grandkids, plus engaging in Church service and community outreach, finding time to write the _RAFT Strategy_ was a challenge. Yet, the purpose kept me going. This message needs to be heard. These strategies need to be read. The Triple Crown Solution needs to be illustrated because the concepts are life changing. To coin a new word; the ideas in this book are epiphamatic.

I guarantee, as you read this book, you'll experience many epiphanies. There is no time to waste, so let's get started on your education right now! You will see as you read that I don't take myself too seriously. Just have fun with it and you will learn a lot while enjoying the journey to a future of financial prosperity.

Acknowledgements

I wish to thank all those who encouraged me to put into print the content of our radio show. I appreciate the patience of all of the Strategic Wealth Coaches (SWCs) in the field. They have been loyal and supportive. I wish to thank my good friend, Debra Shaffer who forced me to sit down and write the first few chapters over a year ago. As she went on to produce her own song, see: www.BlueRosePress.com, which ties in with a wonderful cause. Debra continued needling me until I had enough confidence on my own to propel me forward.

Thank you to the rest of my Team: My third son, Pace Ellsworth, the Director of Program Development at Freedom Financial Radio Network (FFRN), and my personal assistant, was always there to produce the graphs and charts I wanted to illustrate the points. My eldest son, Easton Ellsworth, founder of www.KeyRise.com helped with our website and early editing of the manuscript. He is an important part of our team. My second son, Tanner Ellsworth, a licensed insurance professional who assists with the annual reviews for our policyholders, lit up my life with purpose for getting the book out to our existing and potential clients. And a special thank you to April Ellsworth; who pitched in with a passion as proof reader and compiled the very important glossary of terms.

And lastly, but not leastly, thank you to my darling 4th and 5th borns: Taylor and Jesse-Elyse. You mean the World to me. Your hearts fill me with happiness from your distant collegiate experiences. As I searched and studied, wrote and re-wrote, I felt solidarity with you, knowing you were going through similar growing experiences.

And finally, thank you to my husband Dave, who shares the FFRN stage with me and has supported the effort to get our message out through this much needed book:

<u>*The RAFT Strategy: How to Build Your Tax-Free Nest Egg without Risk.*</u>

Thank you again. I love you all.

Just so YOU know

The information shared in this book is designed to provide general knowledge about current tax advantages and risk free strategies within insurance policies, annuity products, and other asset management vehicles. It is not, however, intended to provide specific legal or tax advice.

Examples within the book are merely illustrations, not guarantees. Recommendations for using the solutions within the book are reserved for State specific licensed insurance, tax, and financial professionals.

The strategies showcased within the book cannot be used to avoid IRS penalties or appropriate taxes. The book does not promote any specific Equity Market investments, Insurance Companies, or Financial Institutions. It is not meant to recommend any specific individual tax plan or arrangement. You are encouraged to consult your, CPA, tax attorney or retirement adviser regarding any of the concepts discussed herein.

Product guarantees are backed by the financial strength and claims paying ability of the issuing insurer, not by the insurance agent or financial adviser. Riders may be available at additional cost. Product and features availability may vary from State to State.

For full details on how life insurance and annuities perform, including fees, expenses and costs of insurance inquire through our website:

www.RAFTstrategy.com

Chapter 1

Your Nest Egg:
Four Phases of Retirement Planning

The turquoise Aruban bay was minutes away, and I had the best view in the house from the fitness room on the starboard bow of the cruise ship. I was fortunate that my treadmill was placed right up against the window. I remember the thought crossed my mind that we had just made it through the last century and things were looking good. Y2K was not the big disaster that everyone had expected. It was Saturday, January 8, 2000, and the S&P 500 had closed on Friday at 1441.47—higher than ever before.

I turned and introduced myself to the gentleman next to me who was laboring on the elliptical machine, "Hi, I'm Laurett, from the DC area, where are you from?" He proceeded to share that he was a lawyer from North Carolina on the verge of retiring a bit earlier than he had expected because "The stock market has been so good to me, beyond my wildest dreams," he said. I can imagine he thought like so many others that he was riding the "Dot Com" rocket ship to infinity. There was no reason to believe that financial calamity was just around the corner. Who knew that the "Tech Bubble" would burst?

I have to be honest; I was riding it too—but in a different way. My position at the time was Director of Program Development for a major network television business news program which aired on ABC in several financial markets including New York, Boston, San Francisco, DC and Chicago. My task was to provide content from the DC market by interviewing the movers and shakers in the technology and bio-tech sectors, alongside traditional businesses that were capitalizing on the booming economy. We produced a program that showcased the success of two or three companies a week. Over a four-year period of time, I interviewed over 600 company executives, including Ernst and Young Entrepreneurs of the Year, lawyers, engineers, project managers, design and advertising firms, even anti-aging experts. You name it. Everyone was on a roll.

Frankly, there were times when I saw the writing on the wall. I would walk into an office ready for an interview, and the CEO would arrive with a nice suntan from weekend escapades on the newly acquired company yacht. Mind you, this was a start-up venture capitalized company, not a well-established Fortune 500 company where vacations were well-deserved. I wondered if the investors really knew how their money was being spent. One question I would typically ask was, "What is your burn rate?" In other words, how much venture capital is your company going through and how fast before this 'dot com' company will get off the ground?"

Sadly, there was a laissez-faire (who-cares) attitude towards the investor's money, because it seemed that all they had to do was get the company to an initial public offering (IPO) and then everyone would be set for life. I knew deep down that I was witnessing a house of cards about to topple, and unless true substance kicked in, the company would implode. However, I was content to hear the stories and convey them in such a way that the audience saw nothing but positive. Still, that feeling of eventual demise was real and true; just a few months later, the Tech Bubble burst. In addition, the tragic events of September 11, 2001 and the loose lending policies that gave rise to the mortgage crises seemed to cause a financial tailspin. Everything came crashing straight down for the next two and one-half years until October 9, 2002, when the S&P 500 hit 776.76.

I often wondered what my lawyer friend from North Carolina was feeling on that day. Was he one of the lucky ones who pulled his money out at the top, or was he like most would-be retirees who watched their IRAs or 401(k)s drop to half? I always say in the business of financial advising that "no one has a crystal ball," so I can only make suggestions based on what we have seen in the past and that history may or may not repeat itself.

You see, America didn't get a break until 2003 when the stock market started to recover and then it took another dive in 2008. It took almost 10 years to recover the losses from the four bear market years that plagued the nation in 2000, 2001, 2002 and 2008. That is why you have often heard 2000 through 2009 referred to as the "lost decade" when it comes to realizing any gains on investments. And now, Bang! . . .Just as most of the losses of 2008 were recovered, 2011 was another bear market year in the S&P. The cycle continues. Where will it end?

Why do I focus on the fluctuations of the stock market? I was not a big investor over the triple-Bear Market years, but I contributed $1000 a month to my Raymond James account, which I saw melt away almost as soon as it was contributed. Of the 36K I placed under management during those years, I was left with only 17K by April of 2003. I remember asking my stockbroker several times if I should take my money out and the answer was always the same: "Just wait it out." He indicated the gains would eventually come, unless I sold my stocks. He would simply say, "It will come back, don't worry about your account." He clearly had no crystal ball and I had no POM POM (Plenty of Money, Peace of Mind). He couldn't tell me when or if the market would come back. In the meantime, 'just waiting it out' meant that I was unable to lock in any of my gains, when they did come, and uncertainty was ever present. It was very confusing. If I kept my money in the market I might lose it and if I sold to lock in the gains, I could miss out on potential growth. It made my head spin and surely didn't make for a good night's sleep.

When I learned about the RAFT Strategy several years ago, I was impressed that I could show others how they can experience growth linked to the equity markets and never experience losses due to market volatility. I was further impressed that I could show others how to build a tax-free nest egg that could be used for retirement, a child's education, trips or whatever, because the money could be accessed tax-free anytime, unlike a qualified IRA or 401(k) plan. I realized that this well-kept secret could change the lives of millions of Americans. It is the best sleeping pill ever, because utilizing the RAFT Strategy means that I won't wake up in the middle of the night trying to conjecture if the market will go up or down, or to buy or sell, or how much of any leftover earnings could be gobbled up by Uncle Sam. When I learned about how to use the RAFT Strategy, I wanted to get the message out to give others hope for their future.

Here is something I know: We have been deceived when it comes to saving for retirement. When we started in the workforce, we thought that Social Security was actually secure so it made sense that we would contribute a portion of our paycheck towards it. Now we know that Social Security (or should I say *Social Insecurity*) has been referred to as the biggest "Ponzi Scheme" in America. It's easy to compare *Social Insecurity* to the Titanic. Who would book passage on the Titanic knowing they would have only a few good days of decadent cruising before smacking into an iceberg, which would cause the ship to sink to the bottom to the Atlantic in just a few hours?

Who would jump on board knowing that the vessel actually was sinkable and that there were only enough lifeboats for about 50% of the passengers? What is the difference between these two historical events? As I see it, unlike *Social Insecurity*, those who booked passage on the Titanic did not know they would run into trouble. We've known for years that *Social Insecurity* is a sinking ship. That is why we are providing an alternative for you. We don't want you sinking in retirement because you have to pay too much to Uncle Sam or because *Social Insecurity* has not lived up to its promises. We don't want you running out of money because inflation has kicked in, gas prices are through the roof, or because the stock market took another dive. Ask yourself: Does your 401(k) look more like a 201(k). Is your 401k, really "ok?" If not, you may be able to consider the RAFT Strategy as your true life RAFT.

Have you ever calculated in your mind each step you must take along the way to provide yourself and your family with a respectable retirement nest egg from which to draw? Have you been sucked into the idea that the best and **only** way to prepare for your future is to sock away money into those tax-deferred qualified plans, including but not limited to: IRAs, 401(k)s, TSPs, 403(b)s, 457s and SEPs? Has anyone ever sat down with you and gone over the four phases of retirement planning? Well it's time they did and it starts right here. The four phases include: Contribution, Accumulation, Distribution and Transfer. Let's discuss how to prepare for each and why it is important to engage in each of these phases.

Phase One:

Contribution occurs during the building and preparation years, typically while you are still working. With the advent of Qualified Plans, which ramped up in 1974 with the Individual Retirement Plan (IRA) and took off like wildfire in 1978 when Congress approved 401(k) plans, Americans began to embrace the concept of tax deferral. This means that income on funds placed into their Qualified Plans would be allowed to grow and compound without being taxed, until it is withdrawn. According to IRS guidelines (as of the date this book was published), the magic age to begin withdrawing the cash from a qualified account without a 10% penalty is 59 ½. Currently, the account owner **must** start taking Required Minimum Distributions (RMD) by age 70 ½. Otherwise, the owner will suffer a 50% tax penalty on the account portion that the IRS deemed to be the required minimum distribution (RMD) for that year.

What is the major motivation behind contributing to one of these qualified plans? The answer is simple: Americans typically believe that they will be in a higher tax bracket while in the workforce than when they retire. Therefore, shifting money towards a qualified plan postpones income tax until distributions begin; which is usually planned for the retirement years. (On the radio show, we often refer to tax-deferred as 'tax procrastination'.) So the concept is to pay less tax during the contribution years when the tax bracket is projected to be higher. This is possible because one does not have to pay the annual income tax on the portion that has been contributed to their qualified plan until they take distributions, typically after age 59 ½.

Many employers provide a 'match', which is a contribution from the company of up to a certain percent of the amount that the employee contributes to the 401(k). For example, when you contribute 5% of your earnings to your 401(k), your company may contribute 5% as well. Both of the contributions are tax-deferred, as is the interest that the account gains from year to year. Some companies will match ½ of your contribution meaning when you contribute 6%, they will pitch in 3% to your 401(k) account. Some companies don't provide a 'match' at all, yet allow their employees to fund their 401(k) so the employee can take advantage of the tax deferred growth. According to IRS guidelines, there are limits to how much of one's income can be saved in qualified accounts like 401(k)s, IRAs, TSP, 403(b) and still experience tax deferred growth. Be sure you find out what your limits are before placing money into your tax-deferred account so you are not blindsided by a taxable event.

Companies help fund qualified plans for their employees partially because they also receive tax advantages for contributing to employees' retirement accounts. And from the employees' standpoint, who wouldn't want to take advantage of the "free" money their employer is providing? This all sounds so great. . .almost too good to be true. Yet, keep in mind that there are strings attached to contributing to qualified plans. (We will address these 'strings' in chapter 4.) For example, most employers do not allow access to money that has accumulated in the company-sponsored retirement program, until the money is "vested" after a certain number of years, or until the employee no longer works for the company. Also, the IRS imposes a penalty for early withdrawal, which is prior to age 59 ½. However, the money tucked away in these qualified plans can be accessed prior to age 59 ½ without a 10% penalty for certain specified reasons, including but not limited to: first time home buying, costs related to education, and medical expenses.

The above paragraphs outlined some of the parameters associated with qualified retirement plans, so you are informed. However, explaining the full details of qualified plans is not the goal of this book. Please consult with your tax-adviser to understand how to adhere to the most up-to-date IRS guidelines.

You may be asking yourself, "What about contributing to a Roth IRA or a Roth 401(k)?" I don't want to ignore the Roth IRA because frankly, I like it the best of all the qualified plans. Here are the reasons: 1) the contributions are taxed at regular income tax rates, 2) accumulation within the account grows tax-free, and 3) distributions are made tax-free. I liken this to paying tax on the seed, not the harvest. Think about it. Here's a scenario: If you were a successful cotton farmer in a 35% tax bracket, and you were given the choice to pay tax on the $100 you spent for your cotton seeds to plant this year or pay tax on your entire harvest, what would *you* choose to do?

Before you answer, let me do the math for you. We know that in a 35% tax bracket, you would owe the government $35 on that planting seed. Now, provided that locusts (rising inflation) did not swarm down and eat up all your seed or a hurricane (volatile stock market) didn't blow through and devastate your crop or there wasn't a drought (soaring unemployment), your harvested cotton crop would sell for roughly $5000 and your tax burden on that $5000 would be about $1750. So you were right; you'd save $1715 by paying tax on the seed, instead of the harvest.

The only qualified retirement plans that work like the cotton farmer who paid tax on the seed instead of the harvest are a Roth IRA and Roth 401(k). Still, there are strings attached to the Roth plans as well. There are limits to how much one can contribute, and the limits do not allow for a very aggressive contribution schedule. Typically, contributions are capped at $6000 annually, and some individuals in higher tax brackets are not allowed to contribute at all.

It is because we love the concept of paying on the seed, and not on the harvest, that we are very passionate about sharing the RAFT Strategy with you. So keep on reading. The pieces of the puzzle will fall into place.

We recognize that qualified plans are not the only way to save for retirement. You can always stuff cash into a mattress or hide it in a can buried in the back yard (which in economic downturn years may actually be preferable to investing in the stock market)! You could buy gold or silver and hope that you bought at the right time, so that your investment will increase in value. You could place your hard-earned cash in an FDIC insured bank, CD, or money market account, which these days yield extremely modest returns. Yes, there are many alternatives, and the purpose of this book is to show you what we believe to be the safest, most efficient nest egg accumulation vehicle available today: The **RAFT** Strategy (**The Retirement Approach Free of Tax**).

Phase Two:

Accumulation can occur simultaneously with the Contribution Phase, or it doesn't have to. Growing the money is the name of the game during the Accumulation Phase; and the faster the better. It is often said that Albert Einstein mused, "The eighth wonder of the world is compound interest." The best accumulation strategies incorporate the miracle of compound interest. The benefit of compound interest compared to simple interest, is that every time interest is applied to the principal or basis, it is locked in and becomes part of a new, higher principal amount. Interest is then gained on the full new principal amount rather that collecting interest on only the original basis, as with simple interest.

Frequently locking in interest gains that become part of your new principal is a key ingredient to mastering the accumulation phase. As stated when we explained the Contribution Phase, tax deferral is definitely superior to being taxed annually on one's income, because it greatly enhances accumulation. (We will show examples and cover the importance of tax- deferral in chapter 4).

According to a Gallup Wellbeing poll of June 2011, 66% of us fear outliving our retirement funds. Additionally, the Employee Benefits Research Institute reported in March of 2011 that 76% of Americans within 5 years of retirement have saved less than $100,000, even though 58% stated they would need at least $250,000 for retirement. That is quite a gap. Their nest egg is not nearly what it needs to be to sustain them through the remainder of their lives. Why is that? Is it because they didn't plan? Is it because they didn't try? Is it because they thought the government was miraculously going to take care of them or the laws would change in their favor? I don't think so.

Consider this: Might there be a fundamental *lack of education* about the importance of being self-reliant? Also, perhaps there is a general lack of understanding of the importance of starting the process early enough so that the accumulative effects of saving, using the most effective vehicles, will truly make a difference.

Because of what I have learned about the various ways to prepare for retirement, I have a passion to share what I believe to be the most efficient ways to accumulate that elusive nest egg. That is what we do on the Freedom Financial Radio Network, which airs throughout the country. And that is also the reason I wrote this book. I firmly believe in the well-known Spanish phrase, "Saber es poder.": Knowledge is power.

We live in a "microwave" society where we have instant access to information and social updates in the forms of Facebook, Twitter and LinkedIn, for example. We are of the disposition that we should not wait for anything. So the principle of delayed gratification is completely lost for those who have not been trained or disciplined themselves to understand the adage that 'good things come to those who wait.'

Recently I encountered a 1970 study by Stanford University professor Walter Mischel of 600 children, all about four and five years old. They were individually provided a large marshmallow and were told that if they waited for just 15 minutes before they bite into it, they would be provided with a second large delicious marshmallow to consume along with the first. Interestingly, only 25% of the children had the self-discipline to wait, even though the payoff would have been double. Well, it's time to save up for double marshmallows, folks. I want you to be the first in line, by learning how to set up your retirement account in a way that it will compound tax-free and without risk.

It has been said that people will go to greater lengths to avoid pain than to achieve pleasure. Because of the inherent penalties for early withdrawal on qualified plans, we may be more motivated to stay with the program rather than incur a penalty by tapping into our retirement fund prematurely for optional purposes, like going on a cruise or buying a new luxury car. For this reason, I respect the incentive for sticking to a qualified plan—yet what if you could have all the benefits of a qualified plan, such as a Roth IRA, without the limitations? What if you knew that your nest egg was safe and that even if the stock market took a dive, you would not lose a penny due to market volatility? What if you could have access to your money without penalty, even before age 59 ½? We will show you how you can have *all of those benefits* with the RAFT Strategy.

Phase Three:

Distribution occurs when one is retired and uses their nest egg for everyday living expenses. Our desire is that both the Contribution and Accumulation Phases have been sufficient to provide enough money to live on during the Distribution Phase. There are two primary categories of distribution, taxable and non-taxed, or in other words: tax-deferred income and income tax-free. We will differentiate between these two types of accounts in Chapter Four by providing two simple illustrations based on building a $1,000,000 retirement account tax-deferred vs. one built free of taxation. You will see that the tax-free distributions can yield up to 50% more income than tax-deferred.

We will show you how you can have income throughout your retirement years, into perpetuity, and still leave a legacy for your beneficiaries; all tax-free. The goal is to have more to spend during retirement because you do not have to give Uncle Sam a cut. As long as the account has been properly designed and funded during the Contribution Phase, the Distribution Phase can give you access to your nest egg totally tax-free. Herein lays the magic of the RAFT Strategy.

Because many of you already have a majority of your future retirement tied up in qualified accounts, I want to give you a bit of comfort. I will describe how you can access that money with minimal tax consequences for you and your legacy, while literally extracting multiple times more from your qualified accounts by using the "AAA Approach," which is explained in chapter 9.

We have a goal to help you understand how to utilize each of the three retirement vehicles that we describe as the "Triple Crown Solution" of safe investing. Keep in mind that these are general principles we are sharing. In order to set up any of these accounts properly, it requires specialized software and expertise from a licensed and trained financial specialist. On the Freedom Financial Radio Program we call them our Strategic Wealth Coaches or SWCs. Please contact our office should you need a referral for a qualified SWC. We educate and work with hundreds of advisers throughout the country, and are here to guide you to those who have the knowledge and expertise to help *you*.

Phase Four:

Transfer occurs when one passes away and the remainder of their retirement nest egg goes to their beneficiaries, typically their children or other family members, a charity or a trust.

There are a large variety of sentiments concerning the Transfer Phase. I have personally met with hundreds of individuals, and I have been amazed to see the broad diversity of ideas that exist in relation to this very emotional stage of life, or death, if you **will** (no pun intended). Some people plan on leaving a lot of money to their family or a charity, even though it may limit their own lifestyle. Others want to spend every last dime while they are still living. Some scrimp and save for retirement so they can enjoy their golden years—only to find out they do not have the slightest idea how to spend money so they end up continuing their frugal lifestyle and perhaps missing out on the dreams they shored up long ago.

Many end up not enjoying the Accumulation Phase years or the Distribution Phase, and perhaps ultimately transfer more to their heirs than they would like. Others go hog-wild and burn through their retirement nest egg so quickly they have to depend on friends and family or heaven forbid—the government—to sustain them, and have nothing left to transfer.

There is no right or wrong attitude about the Transfer Phase of the remainder of your retirement nest egg. Just keep in mind that you do have control as long as you have thought about this important phase in advance. Most importantly, *you* must feel comfortable with your decision to transfer whatever wealth is left, or nothing at all. We simply want to point out that you have a choice to transfer any remaining nest egg to your heirs either tax-deferred or tax-free. It is *your* choice. We will help educate you about how you can do either by utilizing the three different components of the 'Triple Crown Solution of Risk-Free Investing.'

The fact remains that most individuals have less tax deductions in their retirement years than they do in their earning years for a variety of reasons. They may have paid off their home mortgage, thus no tax deduction there. Their children have likely grown and moved out, and are successfully paying their own mortgages & taxes and building their own nest eggs. Also, retirees who have created only tax-deferred accounts are relegated to paying regular state and federal income tax on 100% of their withdrawals. I frequently interview retirees who comment that they are surprised at how much tax they pay every year. They say they had always been taught to defer their income tax because they would be in a lower tax bracket in retirement. Many retirees have shared with me that because they are heavily invested in qualified plans, and have less tax deductions, lower tax rates have eluded them. And now that the Bush Tax Cuts era has expired, we are all paying a larger percentage to Uncle Sam. Now is the time to create a *tax-free* retirement vehicle for your future and the RAFT Strategy is the perfect make and model.

The following illustrates the tax treatment of each of the four phases:

The Four Phases of Retirement Planning

STAGES OF RETIREMENT PLANNING	*IRA/401(k)*	*RAFT*
CONTRIBUTION	Tax Favored	Taxed
ACCUMULATION	Tax Favored	Tax Free!
WITHDRAWAL	Taxed	Tax Free!
TRANSFER	Taxed	Tax Free!

Is postponing taxes really a good idea? Your benefits will be taxable at retirement and likely at a higher tax rate! Which would you choose?

Now that you are aware of the four phases of retirement planning, let's see how well you are doing compared to the rest of the country, according to the 2013 retirement confidence survey conducted by the Employee Benefits Research Institute (EBRI):

Working Individuals' Household Savings:

The chart below comes directly from the EBRI report and shows total household savings and investments accumulated by people still working. In the table directly below the chart, data shows the percentage of American workers who have saved less than $25K, $100K and $250K.

Total Household Savings and Investments Reported by Workers:

Total Savings:	2003	2008	2009	2010	2011	2012	2013
Less than $25,000	55%	49%	52%	54%	56%	60%	57%
Less than $100,000	81%	73%	75%	77%	76%	80%	76%
Less than $250,000	92%	88%	87%	88%	90%	91%	88%

As the report notes, **57% of workers had savings of less than $25,000 in 2013** and only 12% had savings of $250,000 or more. The survey also found that 61% of workers say they will need more than $250,000 in retirement, so there is quite a gap to close.

Another way of thinking about this is to consider the median household savings for workers. These figures show the average savings, which is equivalent to the 50% point for contribution and accumulation. Shockingly, almost 60% of workers have less than $25,000 saved so we can surmise that $25,000 is the average American nest egg for non-retired individuals.

Retired Individuals' Household Savings:

The table below tells the story from the perspective of retirees. We saw above that 57% of workers had less than $25,000 saved, yet it's even more shocking to see that 55% of *retired* households have less than $25,000 in savings. What a precarious state to be in during the Golden Years.

Total Household Savings and Investments for Retirees:

Total Savings:	2003	2008	2009	2010	2011	2012	2013
Less than $25,000	54%	60%	56%	56%	54%	55%	55%
Less than $100,000	74%	75%	78%	73%	71%	72%	73%
Less than $250,000	87%	88%	88%	88%	83%	84%	83%

One of the warnings the report mentions is that while more people expect to work in retirement, few actually do. Making up for inadequate savings with part-time work in retirement just may not be an option. Did you consider how you are doing in comparison with the rest of the country? Are you on the road to success?

We want to help you get there through the strategies we recommend in this book and on our radio program, which airs in many markets throughout the country. We have a Strategic Wealth Coach (SWC) who serves your area, and in fact, it may be your SWC who shared this book with you. Your SWC can provide illustrations of how these strategies work and advise you according to your personal situation; completely complimentary. It doesn't matter how you learn about the Triple Crown Solution to retirement planning. It just matters that you are open to getting educated, which will put you on the track to success.

To get in touch with a SWC, if you do not already have one, be sure to visit our website: www.RAFTstrategy.com. The next chapter will showcase some key elements to achieving your financial goals for retirement. It will get you started on the track to winning your financial race against time, as you secure your Triple Crown to a successful retirement.

Chapter 2

The Triple Crown of Sound Investing: Safety, Liquidity, and Rate of Return

I n the sport of horse racing, the horse that wins all three of the sport's most prestigious events (the Kentucky Derby, the Preakness, and the Belmont Stakes) in a given year is said to have won the Triple Crown.

Undoubtedly, the most famous Triple Crown winner of all time was Secretariat because no other horse has ever clinched the final race with such a wide margin of 31 lengths. It has also been said that a horse race is 'the most exciting two minutes in sports.' All the elements have to be there for the same horse to emerge as the winner time and time again. As of the writing of this book, there have only been 11 Triple Crown Winners, and only 46 horses who have won 2 of the 3 Triple Crown Races.

I can personally attest to the excitement of the experience because my husband and I witnessed **I'll Have Another** win the 137th Preakness just 2 weeks after he won the Kentucky Derby in 2012. There is nothing like watching a perfect specimen earn those flowers.

After Secretariat's death in 1989, the veterinarian who performed the final examination of the horse, Dr. Thomas Swerczek, head pathologist at the University of Kentucky, did not weigh Secretariat's heart, but said, "We just stood there in stunned silence. We couldn't believe it. The heart was perfect. There were no problems with it. It was just this huge engine."

In 1993, Swerczek also performed an examination on Sham, the horse that came in second to Secretariat in each of the three Triple Crown Races in 1973. Swerczek weighed Sham's heart, and it was 18 pounds. Based on Sham's measurement, and having examined both horses, he estimated that Secretariat's heart probably weighed 22 pounds, or about two-and-three-quarters times as large as that of the average horse.

When I learned that the famous Triple Crown winner, Secretariat, had a heart that was two-and-three-quarters times the size of the heart of the average horse, it struck me that there are always several factors contributing to the success of a winner in any arena. In the case of Secretariat, those factors were: strength, stability, speed and stamina—largely stemming from that huge healthy heart of his.

Part of the anatomy of a Triple Crown winner is having a heart that can sustain the horse during those 'most exciting two minutes in sports'. An extremely healthy heart is paramount because horses' hearts have been known to burst during a race when the horse was pushed beyond its limits.

You ask, "Laurett, How does this relate to our retirement accounts?"

Well, the last thing we want to do is set ourselves up for success only to find out that the retirement racehorse we thought we had could not withstand the pressure of inflation, taxes and market volatility. (These will be covered more thoroughly in chapter 3.)

When we look at winning investments, we are basically looking for the same elements of strength, stability, speed and stamina, although they may be worded differently. The elements of a winning investment are: safety, liquidity, rate of return (RoR) and the bonus, as discussed in Chapter One, is tax-free growth, distribution and transfer. Just as Triple Crown winner Secretariat had a large heart which contributed to his overall strength, stability, speed and stamina, we will show you that as investments go, the RAFT Strategy has the biggest heart of all.

As I mentioned, in order to win the Triple Crown, Secretariat had to conquer three races: the Kentucky Derby, the Preakness and the Belmont Stakes. Endurance was critical. He had to go the long haul. He had to maintain excellent condition to finish the first race, and run again with no debilitating injuries or mishaps, so he could compete two more times. That is why his safety was so critical. You better believe that the owners, trainers and jockeys did their best to keep their investment safe from harm. They knew that calculating an exact plan of action for Secretariat to remain free from injury or mishap would pay off because he had the capability to win the Triple Crown. If they could get him safely through the races, while utilizing every bit of his talent and passion, they would get an amazing rate of return (RoR.)

How would you feel if you had a racehorse that you knew could not lose, even in the toughest competition? Well, you do have access to a racehorse of an investment strategy with those very same characteristics. It is called the RAFT Strategy, which utilizes a properly designed and funded Equity Indexed Universal Life (EIUL) insurance policy. It is designed to guarantee against any losses. In fact, the **growth** is tied to the increases of the equity markets, meaning a selected choice of investment indices, like the S&P 500, the DOW, or the Financial Times Stock Exchange 100 (FTSE 100). Growth is emphasized because the investment is only linked to increases in the market, not to decreases. That means that your investment is safe from losing, and gains are locked in automatically every year on the policy's anniversary date!

There is another element of **safety** within the RAFT Strategy. Once your money is safely tucked away in this vehicle, most state laws provide for protection against lawsuits of funds within the EIUL. And lastly, the EIUL is actually a type of life insurance. As a result, the insured's beneficiaries are protected against loss of the policy owner, which is another safety feature.

Are there other safe investments out there? Yes, there are; CDs (Certificates of Deposit), money market accounts and US treasury bills. Still, have you seen the RoRs on those investments? These days the returns don't even keep pace with inflation, given the modest interest that is paid in those accounts. According to mathematical illustrations over the past 30 years, the RAFT Strategy has experienced an 8%-9.5% average rate of return—and the return is *tax-free*. Did you hear me? Let me repeat what this means. I'm not talking about a *good* RoR, like 5 or 6 %. I'm talking about a *great* RoR of 8%-9.5%, compounded, tax-free growth; which you can access completely free of federal, state and local income tax. We are here to share with you a way to have your cake and eat it too. . . safety alongside growth. Based on previous performance, we've picked the winning race horse. Now, you have the opportunity to not only bet on it, but own it, too.

Now let's talk a bit about **liquidity.** Most accounts that we set up for retirement purposes are not liquid to us without a penalty before age 59 ½. They are tax-deferred, but not liquid. Investments that are considered liquid are money in stocks, bonds and savings accounts, yet some are not very safe; even risky. Other investments, like real estate, business ownership and equity in homes are not very liquid because there is a process involved in accessing the money from non-liquid assets. The RAFT Strategy gives us the ability to access our money whenever we need it.

How would you feel knowing that your money is **safe**? Also, would you be happy to know that your nest egg is **liquid** so you have continual access to it? And additionally, what if you knew that your investment strategy has historically received a *great* **rate of return** which could be accessed tax-free? Could knowing that all three of these elements are in place with your retirement nest egg enable you to sleep better at night? I call that POM POM: Plenty of Money & Peace of Mind. Apart from running and winning our own race by having passion for life, I think comfort and security are up there with the things that people value the most. Hurray for POM POM!

Our office conducts several hundred account reviews every year for existing clients and I hear this all the time, "Thank you for leading me to this strategy, because I never have to worry that my money is going to take a huge dive when the stock market does." That's what we do folks; educate our listeners on how to get the upside of the Market and not the downside. I often refer to the stock market as the 'shock market' because nobody likes to go into shock when they open their statement or get online only to see their assets have been zapped away at the mercy of the volatile Market. I think we all agree that Will Rogers was right on track when he said, "I'm more concerned with the return *of* my money than the return *on* my money." At the end of the day, it's not how much money we make, but how much money we keep.

I'm talking about safety here, folks. Ask yourself how important it is to you. If you are not quite sure, let me give you a formula to help you out. It's called the "Rule of 100." It means that whatever age you are equals the same percentage of your nest egg that you ought to be sure is in a safe, non-risk position. For example: at 40 years old, at least 40% of your assets should be in safe investments. The other 60% could be placed in more aggressive investment strategies that are not necessarily risk-free, yet have a potential for stronger gains. This is because you have more time than a 65-year-old, for example, to make up any losses prior to retiring. The older we get, the less we can afford to have any risk factor at all. Although in my mind, if I can have *great potential for growth without any risk*, I've got the best of both worlds. It's like betting on a horse without the possibility of losing, and the gain depends only on how many lengths he wins by. The more lengths = the stronger the return. Secretariat was quite a safe bet, as is the RAFT Strategy. We've briefly discussed how this properly designed and funded EIUL has proven to be safe, now let's check it out for **liquidity**.

When Secretariat was deemed a promising specimen, the owners immediately recognized the potential fortune of syndicating his breeding rights. In addition to the money Secretariat's owners won through racing, they earned millions though liquidating his assets. They simply provided the offspring of a proven winner to horse enthusiasts and investors who hoped to capitalize on the Secretariat legacy.

Although Secretariat earned over 155K for his Derby win (equal to about 760K today), that amount paled in comparison to the 190K that Secretariat's owners were assured to earn every time he was bred. This insured flexibility as well as resiliency to the investment. And that 190K was guaranteed before Secretariat had even notched his first victory as a three-year-old, which resulted in a record breaking six million syndication deal. His total syndication revenues amounted to over 30 million in today's terms. In other words, not to be "racy" here folks, but the syndication rights to breed Secretariat were literally converted to liquid assets.

The primary reason we contribute to our nest egg is to prepare for the future, and yet we all recognize that there will be emergencies and eventualities that pop up throughout the years. Along with **safety**, we want **liquidity** because we want to know we can have access to our own money whenever we need it. What do we do when we need an extra 10K for our daughter's wedding, or an extra few thousand to fund our kid's education? Just knowing that we have this access gives us that POM POM we are all after. The RAFT Strategy is set up to allow us to have access to our nest egg whenever we need it with little or no penalty. In comparison, we don't have to worry about avoiding a 10% penalty by waiting until we're 59 ½ to take distributions, as with a tax-qualified plan like an IRA or a 401(k). Once we know our nest egg is safe from loss and that we can have access to it when we need it. Our main concern is that it will grow enough to provide for our needs down the road. So how can we be sure we will get the RoR we deserve? Read on.

According to National Underwriter Magazine, 72% of adults fear outliving their income. It's no mystery when we see five out of 11 years; as in 2000, 2001, 2003, 2008 and 2011, which all experienced devastating losses. The average bear market lasts for 18 months, and typically takes 5.2 years to recover the losses. That's almost seven years from start to finish. Ask yourself, "How many seven-year periods do I have left in my lifetime to play the 'shock' market game?"

I know, I know, your financial adviser tells you that the average **rate of return** is 7.3% over the past 100 years. And technically they are correct, yet they have not told you the whole truth. Just remember this: The same percentage increase on a lower base does not equal the increase on a higher base. I'll tell you folks, I'm not impressed with *average* rates of returns because we can only spend *compound* returns.

So what is the difference between *compound* returns and *average* returns? This is best answered with an example: Let's just say you invested 100 dollars in the 'shock' market and that investment lost 50% of its value, then you would be left with 50 dollars. Most money managers would say "Hang on, you rode the market down, now ride it back up!" But here's the problem: Your account just lost 50%. You might think, "Hey, my account just lost 50%, now I can just watch it gain 50% and it will be back to my principal amount of 100 dollars." Well friends, that's wrong. Gaining 50% on your new 50 dollar base would only increase your account to 75 dollars. So, the compound effect of the fall and rise in the market of 50% results in a 25% decrease in your modest nest egg.

To make the point that average returns are not the same as real (or compound) returns even more clear; let's say that the sun, moon, and stars all lined up with Mother Nature along with the stock market and your investment increased 100% in one year. That would be amazing, right? Now let's see what happens if that same account then decreased 50% the following year. In real numbers you would see a $100,000 investment climb to $200,000 and then fall back to $100,000. Repeating the process for the next 2 years would place your account, once again, exactly where you started out, right? You made 0% on your investment over that 4 year period of time. Those results are called compound return. Yet, if you asked money managers, they might say your average return was 25%. Isn't that confusing?

To take this scenario a step further, look at what happens to your investment if it is protected on the downturn years. In year two and four, when your investment took a 50% loss, your account remained where it ended the years before each loss. Your $100,000 base will have turned into $200,000 the 1st year, waited out the 2nd year, doubled again to $400,000 the 3rd year, and remained at $400,000 in year four. The following table will make this concept even clearer.

Market Performance	Average Rate of Return	Compound or Real Return	Principal Protected Rate of Return
Initial investment	$100,000	$100,000	$100,000
+100%	= $200,000	$200,000	$200,000
-50%	= $100,000	$100,000	No Loss
+100%	= $200,000	$200,000	$400,000
-50%	= $100,000	$100,000	No Loss
Total % Return	100/4= 25%	0%	400%

Does this make sense to you? Do you see how compound returns are not the same as average returns? In fact, a Dalbar Study in 2003 indicated that over the past 100 years, the typical equity investor only earned an average of 2.57% annually. This is because of the compounding effect of the increases and decreases of the stock market. So really, your total increase is not likely the average 7.3% your stockbroker may have told you, but actually less than a 3% rate of return. No wonder we have had a tough time making great RORs in the market!

How would you like to know that your "average" returns *are the same as* your "compound" returns? This is only possible if our accounts solely experience *gains* from the market—and never losses. In other words, the RAFT Strategy has Principal Protection when the market is down, and when the Market increases, the gains are locked in every year and become a part of our principal.

Pay attention to the following example of a 3-year period of Principal Protection and Lock in of the gains as compared with traditional market volatility. Notice that the investment is starting with $100,000. When the **SHOCK** Market experienced a 10% gain the first year, the new principal is locked in at $110,000. In year two, when the market fell 10%, the Principal was protected and remained locked in at its highest level of $110,000. In year three, as the Market rose again by 5%, the principal gained and locked in that 5% increase, yet again. Keep in mind, there are only two things that will happen in the cash account of the RAFT from year to year. It will either remain the same as the previous year or protect your account against losses in the Market or, it will gain according to the parameters of the policy, which usually means it will lock in gains up to a cap (contracted maximum rate).

Principal Guarantee: Lock-in & Reset

Gains become new principal

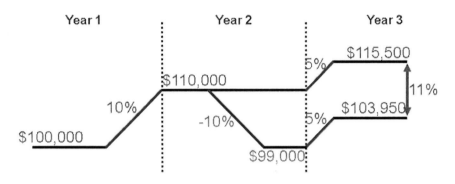

That is a $11,550 difference because of the annual lock in and reset.

This is what the RAFT Strategy has to offer: principal guarantee combined with the maximum cap on gains. Since the RAFT Strategy is a properly designed and funded EIUL (remember this means equity indexed universal life) contract with an established, top-rated insurance company, it offers this principal guarantee. This means the account is measured every year on its anniversary date. **When the *SHOCK* market suffers losses, your principal is protected!** When the market gains, interest is credited to your account according to the index strategy selected up to a certain capped amount. The additional amount is now locked in as your new principal. Let's say, for example that your RAFT had a cap of 16%. This means that when the index to which it is linked rises, your gain that year will be up to 16%. Your account will lock in 100% of the gains of the equity markets, according to the parameters of the policy. Should the market gain beyond 16% in a given year, your account would increase by 16%, and the gains would become part of your new principal.

You may wonder how this is possible—how can a company guarantee against losses while providing such a great **rate of return?** We're talking about a proven race horse here. The insurance companies we recommend that provide the EIULs are solvent and viable, and many have existed for over 100 years. Later in this book, it will be explained as to how insurance companies can protect our money while giving us a great rate of return. And as a bonus, distributions can be accessed *tax-free*.

Remember the magic of winning a race is to choose the right horse: one with strength, stability, speed and stamina. The magic of building a winning nest egg is to choose an adviser who has access to the best companies and products and will act in your best interest. And finally, not to beat a dead horse. . .I just wanted you to visually remember that the three most important elements to a great investment are **safety, liquidity,** and a great **rate of return.** Should you forget—just remember Secretariat.

See the Risk/Return Option Bubbles and chart below which illustrate several types of investments and how closely they meet the criteria of the Triple Crown of Sound Investing: **Safety, Liquidity and Rate of Return.**

The Risk/Return Options

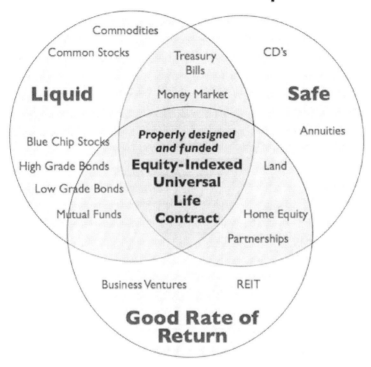

We are all aware of many types of investment and what features and benefits they possess. I agree with many other financial professionals that the RAFT Strategy is the one vehicle that potentially possesses all three of these important characteristics, and as a bonus, it delivers tax-free distributions as well.

Investment	Safety	Liquidity	Rate of Return
EIUL	X	X	X
Annuities	X	Partial	Moderate
CDs	X		Modest
Money Market	X		Modest
Treasury Bills	X		Modest
Mutual Funds		X	Possible
Bonds		X	Possible
Stocks		X	Possible
Commodities		X	Inconsistent
Business Ventures			Possible
Limited Partnerships			Possible
Land	X		Inconsistent
Real Estate	X		Inconsistent
Fixed Annuities	X	Partial	Modest
Variable Annuities		Partial	Possible
Fixed Indexed Annuities	X	Partial	Moderate

In order to see how the RAFT Strategy may work for you, please contact our office to have a specialized illustration designed based on your life. We take many factors into consideration like: your age, gender, health status, when you want to retire, and how many years we have to prepare. We plug all that information into a software system which calculates exactly what your Tax-Free distributions could be. The illustration we provide is totally free of charge and can give you great insight while you take control of your future.

You may request a complimentary illustration through our website: *www.RAFTstrategy.com*

Chapter 3

Eliminating the Risks to Your Nest Egg: Market Volatility, Taxes, Inflation

Linda and Nathan sat down to read and flip through the morning paper with a familiar cup of decaf. They opened up to the financial section and noticed that some of their investments in the market were not performing well. In fact, one of the technology stocks Nathan had been watching in particular had dropped about 5% three days in a row, then it spiked 10% on the 4th day and stayed steady for a few days. But this week the stock continued decreasing again, little by little.

Suddenly it struck him. He looked over at Linda and mused. . . "Linda, remember in the late 90s, we couldn't miss—every stock that we invested in grew? But this; this is torture! Every week I go online and watch our stocks go up and down—It's driving me crazy! We're never going to be able to retire. We had $375 thousand last year in this IRA and now it's down to $300 thousand. We're going to outlive our money. I never thought I'd regret being so dog-gone healthy. Dr. Weiss told me my chances to hit near 100 are pretty good since Grandma Sarah lived to be 97. What are we going to do?"

Linda thought back to the 1980s when she and Nathan were getting 12% return on their CDs. "I just wish we could get a decent rate without having to take on all this risk. I mean, can't we just get out of the market altogether and place our money someplace where we know it will stay put? Then we could sleep at night without worrying about all these stupid statements!"

The family Maltese jumped into Linda's lap and she reflected to herself. . . . "Thank heavens I buried that ten thousand dollars in a can outside in the far corner of the backyard. . .at least I'll have enough money to pay for dog food as long as the prices don't skyrocket."

"Honey, can we cash in that crazy stock of yours and buy a CD instead?" Linda said.

"Are you serious? We can't get more than 2% tops in a CD right now" Nathan snipped. Linda piped back, "Well, it's better than losing money and stressing out every day!" Linda felt her blood pressure rising. Tomorrow was Valentine's Day and she did not want to be thinking about finances at all. Was she going to get the traditional box of chocolates? She hoped they were going to that fancy restaurant with the waterfront view and the lobster tails.

Nathan looked out at the frosty ground. "Oh my Gosh!" he thought, "Taxes are due in two months." His mind raced to his IRA again and he started fuming. "I have to start taking distributions in five years when I'm 70 ½, and I'm going to be blasted with taxes. I wish I had a way to get all that money out of my retirement account tax-free."

Nathan thought through the last decade of the market volatility. He remembered 2000, 2001 and 2002 which wiped out all his gains he had made in the late 1990s. Then the Market turned around for a solid five years. And just as his retirement account had regained all the losses of those three devastating years, and his principal was once again almost $300,000, 2008 struck and he saw a 35% decrease in his accounts bringing his nest egg back down to $195,000. His mind started swimming, "What was I thinking? I never planned on taking an early retirement and I thought a couple of extra years of working would be enough to save me. Why did I think I could even retire at all?"

Now it was Nathan who reflected back to the 1980s when he was able to make 12% in his CDs. Sure, his mortgage rate was 16%, but somehow it seemed like everything was relative and the impact of the compounded growth he got in his bank account was much more dramatic with a higher interest rate. How could he and Linda ever increase their assets enough to retire when they could only get 1-2% annual rate of return in their CDs and money market accounts; and *that* was taxable?

Linda got up from her cozy armchair and walked over to Nathan. Slipping her arms around his shoulders, she whispered, "I wish we could grow our money without risking it. I just want to know that our nest egg is there for us when we want it so you can stop worrying. I want my happy hubby back."

Nathan and Linda's story illustrates how market volatility, taxes and inflation can threaten to eliminate your nest egg. You're probably thinking "I really don't want to have to think about these things." Who does? We suggest you hang in with us and you will be rewarded by learning how you can escape from these three asset-eating monsters.

First, let's talk about Market Volatility:

What causes the stock market to seemingly swing uncontrollably? Why is it that so often as soon as we think we have picked a winning stock or mutual fund, that same fund is derailed off the mission we had planned for it? Frankly, it is no secret that market volatility is based largely upon the hopes, fears and perceptions of the public. These emotional and intellectual responses pepper our actions, whether or not they are rational. In recent years these have included public perceptions of the "Tech Bubble Burst" 2000-2002, the terrorist attacks of September 11th, 2001 and the housing crisis of 2008.

The following is a list, to name a few, of the things that cause market volatility:

- the state of the economy, both domestic and global
- world events
- wars and conflicts
- industry changes
- natural disasters
- political turmoil or changes
- taxes and subsidies

Like it or not, the average person has little or no control over the above events. We simply try to gauge how they may affect the market and invest accordingly. How long are you going to keep getting sucked into this mentality? Just stop. Hold the phone! We have the solution. What if you never had to worry when the market fell and you could be assured that market increases translated into interest credits to your nest egg?

Take a look at the following chart which depicts the real peaks and valleys of the S&P 500 Index over the last decade from 2000-2010. What if you could only experience the gains in the market and not the losses? Additionally, what if those gains were locked in every year and became your new principal amount? And lastly, what if your principal plus interest experienced compounded growth, without risk? Clearly, you will see the dramatic difference when your account does not experience market declines, even with a 15% cap on gains.

Year	S&P 500 Historical Return	$100,000 Investment	Increases locked in Annually	$100,000 Investment
2000	-10.14%	$89,860	0.00%	$100,000
2001	-13.04%	$78,147	0.00%	$100,000
2002	-23.37%	$59,903	0.00%	$100,000
2003	26.38%	$75,485	15.00%	$115,000
2004	8.99%	$82,202	8.99%	$125,338
2005	3.00%	$84,664	3.00%	$129,098
2006	13.62%	$95,675	13.62%	$146,681
2007	3.53%	$99,021	3.53%	$151,858
2008	-34.12%	$65,233	0.00%	$151,858
2009	23.50%	$80,233	15.00%	$174,636
2010	12.80%	$89,863	12.80%	$196,989
Acct Bal		**$89,863**		**$196,989**
Average RoR	-0.98%	Total Loss for 10 yrs. >10%	7.19%	Total Gain for 10 yrs. = 97%

As you can see from the above illustration, the 10 year historical period average rate of return from the S&P 500 is a net negative of nearly 1% resulting in over a 10% loss. In comparison, look at the total gains locked in annually of 7.19% compounded rate of return, which results in a 97% overall increase.

Now that we've shown you the causes and effects of market volatility, we assure you that the RAFT Strategy can guard against market losses while still allowing you to participate in the market gains. There are several ways insurance companies protect investor's principal while locking in annual gains. An insurance company may do this by pooling together large amounts of money and securing grade corporate bonds which guarantee a fixed rate of 5%, for example. Once the insurance has covered their operating costs, they may take the remainder of the interest and exercise options in stocks and bonds. When the option decreases, they can opt out and guarantee the policy holder's principal. When the options increase, they can lock in the gains.

This book is not intended to go into detail about exactly how insurance companies use puts and calls and actuarial formulas to increase assets. The intent is to assure the reader that the insurance companies are legally obligated to adhere to the contractual guarantees within Equity Indexed insurance products; and the products offered are designed accordingly.

Now let's talk about your Taxes:

Have you ever felt that knot in the pit of your stomach when you thought about all the money Uncle Sam has reserved in your retirement account? Nathan is not the only one who dreads tax time. The Federal government essentially has a permanent tax lien on your qualified accounts. Tax-*Deferral* is very simply 'Tax-*Procrastination*'. As you take distributions on your IRA, 401(k), TSP, or 403(b), 457 or any other type of tax-deferred plan; remember you will be paying regular income tax rates on 100% of the cash you pull out of the account.

Have you ever wondered why the IRS came up with such a grand idea? Answer: The IRS is well paid for their patience. Their asset (your tax burden) grows and compounds more each year you stick with the program. It doesn't take a rocket scientist to figure out that the qualified plans are a great idea for Uncle Sam; yet not such a great idea for us.

To return to our farming analogy, imagine you were a cotton farmer and you were given a choice to either pay income tax on the seed you bought to plant your crop, or to pay income tax on your harvest at the end of the season. Your choice would likely not be very difficult, because the tax on your seed, would be minuscule compared to the tax on your harvest. Let me explain. Suppose you spent $100 on your cottonseed and that year your income tax bracket is at 35%. Well, had you chosen to pay your tax upfront, prior to planting your seed, your tax obligation would be $35.00. Now, if you chose the second option of waiting to pay your taxes on the harvest, you'd be paying much more than $35.00. Let's say your harvest sold for $1000, your tax burden would be $350; 10 times the amount you would have paid on the seed you used to plant the crop!

Do you really think that taxes are going to remain low? "Wait a minute," you might say, "Who says tax rates are low?" Well, they are, comparatively. Have a look at this chart that shows the federal tax rates for over the past century; ever since the tax code began in 1913.

Notice that tax rates have been as high as 94%, during World War II in 1944, and the average rate over the past 100 years has been 61%.

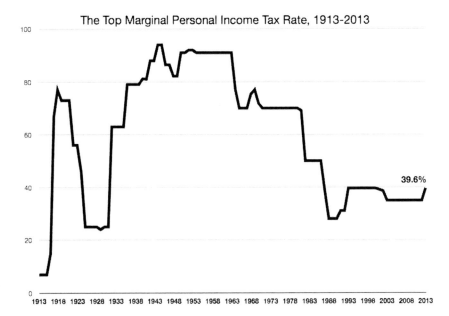

The Top Marginal Personal Income Tax Rate, 1913-2013

In my opinion, taxes are on sale. Even at the current highest rate of 39.6%, they are way lower than the average rate over the past century. I don't see the IRS cutting taxes any time soon; not with the federal deficit, the war on terror, and the economic instability we have been facing.

According to a Gallup poll taken in September 2011, the average American estimates that the federal government wastes 51 cents of every dollar it spends. This is a new high in a Gallup trend question first asked in 1979, up from 38% in 1986. Among other factors, Federal spending is cited as a clear culprit leading to impending tax increases. . .or at least one reason why taxes are not likely to decrease. Polls also indicate that 90% of American taxpayers believe taxes will either stay the same or increase over the next 10 years and beyond. Isn't it time you started building your tax-free nest-egg? Pay the tax on what you can now, let it grow tax-free and when the time comes, you can access the compounded growth tax-free, as well. We'll share with you how The RAFT Strategy can help you do it.

And finally: What about Inflation?

The average rate of inflation over the past 50 years has been close to 4%. Based on that rate of inflation and taking the rule of 72 into account, our cost of living essentially doubles every 18 years. Think about that. Let's say you are 36 years old right now and it seems that you need a minimum of $5000/month to live comfortably. Accounting for inflation, by the time you reach 54 years old, you'll want at least $10,000/month to maintain your lifestyle. When you reach 72 years old, your comfort figure will be about $20,000 a month. You see how that works? Keep that formula in mind when you are looking at how much you and your family will need to get by once you retire.

Now that you know how much you will need to be comfortable in retirement, how about considering which investments are going to keep up with inflation so you won't be getting behind in any year leading up to the time you want to access your retirement funds?

In the previous chapter, we showcased many types of investments. Only three of those possessed the basic elements of a sound investment; safety, liquidity and a good rate of return. Those three investment vehicles are: CDs (Certificates of Deposit), FIAs (Fixed Indexed Annuities), and EIUL (Equity Indexed Universal Life) policies. Historically, there seems to be a correlation between the growth of all three of these investments and the rate of inflation.

Why is that important? Well, because, at a minimum we want to ensure that the increases on our investments outpace inflation. And the hope is that we can get a good Rate of Return (RoR) beyond simply keeping up with the increasing cost of living.

Maybe you feel the same way I do. I don't like inflation any more than the next gal or guy. Yet, if I have to experience inflation I want my investment to be tied to inflation. When the cost of living increases, I want my investments to increase also.

Let's briefly take a look at each of the three investment vehicles, CDs, FIAs, and EIULs to see how the RoR in each stacks up against inflation.

Certificates of Deposit:

A CD is a time deposit issued by a bank or credit union that pays a certain rate of interest for a specified period of time. Most CDs have a fixed-rate, which pays a constant rate of interest for the lifetime of the CD. Although market interest rates may increase or decrease before the maturity date of a given CD, the interest rate on a fixed-rate CD will not change. The length of time we commit to keeping the CD is related to and determines the rate of return the bank offers. The longer the period we intend to hold the CD, the higher the interest rate will be. Holding a CD for a longer period of time introduces the possibility that inflation could outpace the interest earned during that period of time. Additionally, if our CD was locked in at a lower rate, and T-bills increased, our original CD may be relegated to a lower interest rate than a newer CD, thus limiting the rate of return.

While you may like the idea of having a locked-in interest rate on a CD, another concept to consider is that inflation or the expectation of inflation also determines interest rates. For example, periods of high or low rates of inflation are usually associated with relatively high or low rates on Treasury Bills (T-Bills) and CDs. See this chart as an example:

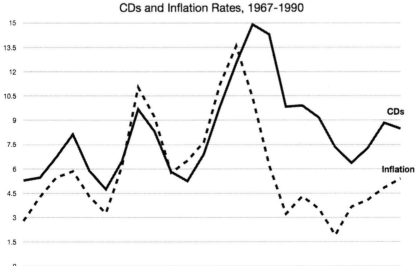

CDs and Inflation Rates, 1967-1990

I look at it like this:

Since the Rates on CDs are tied to T-Bills, and T-Bills tend to follow the trends of the Consumer Price Index (CPI), which in turn is linked to inflation, we cannot count on getting ahead by placing our money in CDs. To make matters worse, the interest gained on CDs is taxed annually, albeit at capital gains rates. Being taxed every year limits the compounding effect within any investment account. That is why utilizing tax-deferred accounts, and better yet, tax-free strategies, like a Roth IRA or the RAFT Strategy may be preferable.

Fixed Indexed Annuities:

In Chapter 7, I will go into greater detail about how Fixed Indexed Annuities (FIAs) are structured. Initially, I just want you to understand that the tax treatment on FIAs is tax-deferred, so more dramatic compounding effects can take place within FIAs, compared to CDs. Additionally, the average RoR over the past 20 years for FIAs has been between 4 and 6%, which is about 1-3% greater than the average rate of inflation and certainly greater than today's (2013) yield on a CD, which is around 1% for a one-year CD. Since the interest in an FIA is added to the account and locked in as principal every year, the compounding effect coupled with the tax-deferred status makes an FIA a stronger investment than a CD. Keep in mind, however that the increases in an FIA will eventually be taxed at the State and Federal level and the entire amount is taxable unless it is opened as Roth.

The owners age is also a consideration when choosing to use and annuities for investing because the IRS may impose a 10% penalty for withdrawing funds prior to age 59 ½. FIAs are safe, yet have limited liquidity even after age 59 ½.

Equity Indexed Universal Life:

According to mathematical calculations, over the past 25 years, the average rate of return within an EIUL has been 7%-9% depending on the policy. Tax-deferred growth and tax-free distributions are earmarks of a properly designed and funded EIUL, as long as the account is set up and accessed properly. We are talking about an investment that yields 3-5 % over the average inflation rate, and that is tax free, so just tack on an extra 10-35% buying power to your total distributions at retirement time.

In summary:

1) The average yield on a CD typically mirrors the rate of inflation, and is taxed annually at capital gains rates.
2) The average annual increase in an FIA has historically shown to be about 2% above the rate of inflation. Increases are locked in annually and tax-deferred. Distributions are taxed at regular income tax rates.
3) The average annual increase in an EIUL has shown to be about 4% above the rate of inflation, and the cash within the policy can be accessed tax-free.

A final word about Risk: The Rule of 100

You may have heard of the Rule of 100. It is a guideline indicating what percentage of one's portfolio should sensibly be exposed to risk, like Market volatility. Simply subtract your age from 100; that is the percentage that most financial advisers would say should sensibly be placed in more aggressive investments that have possibly higher potential for gains, yet are exposed to greater risk. The principle, for example, is that a 35 year old can afford to hold a higher percentage of aggressive investments than can a 60 year old because they are younger and have more time to make up losses, should financial losses occur. So, the 35 year old could sensibly have up to 65% of their investment portfolio in a risk position (100-35=65); whereas, a 60 year old would tolerate a maximum of 40% at risk (100-60=40).

Risk tolerance is an individual preference. Some are born more risk tolerant than others. Some never want to risk a penny. Others may never tire of the roller coaster ride and seek out new roller coasters every day. You decide where you stand, and what percentage of your nest egg you feel comfortable keeping in a risk position. **You** decide when you want to get off the roller coaster ride.

I'm reminded again of the quote often attributed to Will Rogers, "I'm more concerned with the return *of* my money than the return *on* my money." Isn't that so true, even for those risky people? Nobody truly wants to lose their money. I often say on the radio and to our clients that we can help you with the portion of your portfolio you do not want at risk. For some of you, that would be a majority of your retirement nest egg.

Next time you read the financial page to see where the *SHOCK* market stands, just remember that whatever the numbers indicate today, the numbers will change tomorrow, and everyday thereafter. No two days in the *SHOCK* market are ever identical. I don't have to remind you that the volatility in the Markets will likely wreak havoc with your retirement savings. For that reason, we recommend placing a portion of your nest egg into safe investments like CDs, FIAs, and the RAFT Strategy; investments that enable you to sleep at night because you know your money is safe.

I believe there is a place for safe investment strategies in your retirement portfolio and a Strategic Wealth Coach (SWC) can help you determine the correct ratio for you. Provided you have not already engaged an SWC, be sure and contact our information center to be referred to an SWC in your area: www.RAFTstrategy.com

Chapter 4

Tax-Deferred vs. Tax-Free Investing Strings Attached to Qualified Plans

I n one of the world's most beloved fables, Geppetto created hundreds of puppets to entertain and delight the townspeople. As the story goes, one evening, after painting the finishing touches on the face of his newest creation, Geppetto decided to wait until morning to apply the strings to the little wooden boy he called Pinocchio.

For decades, Geppetto had longed for a son, so before climbing into bed, he once again got on his knees and prayed that someday, somehow, he would be given a son of his own. Almost instantly, his workshop filled with blue light from an open window and there appeared the beautiful Blue Fairy. She told Geppetto that his wish of having a son may soon come true.

Thinking that the vision was just a dream, Geppetto fell asleep only to be awakened the next morning by his active little Pinocchio, who was still wooden, yet, very much alive.

We all know how the story unfolds. When we add Jiminy Cricket, 'the conscience' or 'voice of reason' and Stromboli, the evil villain who imprisoned Pinocchio, the scenario metaphorically relates to almost any situation concerning evil vs. good, wrong vs. right, bondage vs. free, and yes, tax-deferred vs. tax-free.

As I see it, qualified, or tax-deferred plans are like puppets with strings attached and the tax-free alternative, the RAFT Strategy is like Pinocchio, who can move without strings. Now, I'm not saying that assessing tax is evil. I'm just saying that given a choice, I am certain, once you see the value of tax-free vs. tax-deferred access to your retirement nest egg, you will undoubtedly prefer tax-free.

Ask yourself, "If I were a wooden puppet, would I rather be controlled by strings and a marionette who gets a piece of the action whenever I dip into my nest egg, or would I rather be Pinocchio, without strings attached, and make up my own retirement dance?"

Now don't worry, even if you choose to go strings free, you don't have to figure out the dance all by yourself; that's where Jiminy Cricket (your Strategic Wealth Coach) comes in. They can give you some education and recommendations, and the good news is that you have a choice; you can listen and take their advice, or you can ignore it. Yet, if you don't learn what the choices are, you are bound by ignorance and you are relegated to continue doing what you have been doing, whether it works or not.

Well, I know that once I start accessing my retirement nest egg, I'd rather dance with no strings and make my own decisions based on results and suggestions from someone who doesn't get a piece of the action. Although, I do not think that the intent of tax-deferral is evil, I do believe that the big winner is the Federal Government, not the taxpayer. You see, I'd rather pay tax on the seed of my investment than the harvest. Uncle Sam was a genius when he came up with the qualified plans, because he will get many times more tax out of us by waiting for it to grow and compound before taking his share.

Let's talk about these strings attached to the qualified plans, like 401(k), IRA, TSP, and 403b plans, to name a few. To set the stage, let's look at a simple example of the compounding effect.

We've all heard the scenario of a dollar doubled every day for 20 days. You know the drill; day one we have $1, day two it multiplies to $2, day three, it becomes $4, and so on. After 20 days of doubling our money every day, we end up with over a million dollars; $1,048,576.00 to be exact.

Now take that same doubling dollar and tax the increase at the current capital gains rate of 15% and an income tax rate of 30%. Still, we are doubling the principal everyday as earned and compounded. What do we end up with?

Let's take a look:

A Dollar Doubled Every Day

Day	Doubled Daily	15% Tax	30% Tax
0	$1.00	$1.00	$1.00
1	$2.00	$1.85	$1.70
2	$4.00	$3.42	$2.89
3	$8.00	$6.33	$4.91
4	$16.00	$11.71	$8.35
5	$32.00	$21.67	$14.20
6	$64.00	$40.09	$24.14
7	$128.00	$74.17	$41.03
8	$256.00	$137.21	$69.76
9	$512.00	$253.83	$118.59
10	$1024.00	$469.59	$201.60
11	$2048.00	$868.74	$342.72
12	$4,096.00	$1,607.17	$582.62
13	$8,192.00	$2,973.26	$990.46
14	$16,384.00	$5,500.53	$1,683.78
15	$32,768.00	$10,175.97	$2,862.42
16	$65,536.00	$18,825.55	$4,866.12
17	$131,072.00	$34,827.27	$8,272.40
18	$262,144.00	$64,430.44	$14,063.08
19	$524,288.00	$119,196.32	$23,907.24
20	**$1,048,576.00**	**$220,513.19**	**$40,642.31**

Can you believe our grand total at the end of 20 days increase on our money taxed at 15% is just $220,513.92? Even worse. . . look at the havoc wreaked by the 30% tax! We end up with only $40,642.31. That's a far cry from the Million Dollar Nest Egg we were hoping for.

I know this is an extreme example and we could never expect or plan on a 100% increase on our money every day, or even every year, for that matter. But I hope this little illustration instills in you the notion that taxing your gains as earned is not the way to go.

Now let's take a look at a more realistic way of getting to $1 million in a scenario utilizing an 8% annual rate of return. Why 8%? Well, I will be showing you in Chapter 5 & 6 how the RAFT Strategy has historically produced an 8-9.5% rate of return over the past 25 years. So, to be on the conservative end, let's keep the figures down to an 8% annual interest increase. Assuming a $100,000 after tax investment and no other contributions, again we are showing the compounding effect with:

1.) 0% annual tax on gains

2.) 15% annual rate (akin to capital gains tax)

3.) 30% taxed annually on gains (closer to income taxes)

Check it out:

Compounded Growth – 30 year plan – Taxed Annually

Year	0% Tax	15% Tax	30% Tax
0	$100,000.00	$100,000.00	$100,000.00
1	$108,000.00	$106,800.00	$105,600.00
2	$116,640.00	$114,062.40	$111,513.60
3	$125,971.20	$121,818.64	$117,758.36
4	$136,048.90	$130,102.31	$124,352.83
5	$146,932.81	$138,949.27	$131,316.59
6	$158,687.43	$148,397.82	$138,670.32
7	$171,382.43	$158,488.87	$146,435.86
8	$185,093.02	$169,266.11	$154,636.26
9	$199,900.46	$180,776.21	$163,295.89
10	$215,892.50	$193,068.99	$172,440.46
11	$233,163.90	$206,197.68	$182,097.13
12	$251,817.01	$220,219.12	$192,294.57
13	$271,962.37	$235,194.03	$203,063.06
14	$293,719.36	$251,187.22	$214,434.60
15	$317,216.91	$268,267.95	$226,442.93
16	$342,594.26	$286,510.17	$239,123.74
17	$370,001.81	$305,992.86	$252,514.67

18	$399,601.95	$326,800.38	$266,655.49
19	$431,570.11	$349,022.80	$281,588.20
20	$466,095.71	$372,756.35	$297,357.14
21	$503,383.37	$398,103.78	$314,009.13
22	$543,654.04	$425,174.84	$331,593.65
23	$587,146.36	$454,086.73	$350,162.89
24	$634,118.07	$484,964.63	$369,772.01
25	$684,847.52	$517,942.22	$390,479.25
26	$739,635.32	$553,162.30	$412,346.08
27	$798,806.15	$590,777.33	$435,437.46
28	$862,710.64	$630,950.19	$459,821.96
29	$931,727.49	$673,854.80	$485,571.99
30	$1,006,265.69	$719,676.93	$512,764.02

Keep in mind that a Tax-Deferred investment as in an IRA or 401(k) on $100,000, gathering 8% compound interest would yield the same $1,006,265.69. Yet, the gains would be subject to regular income tax, bringing your nest egg down significantly, depending on your tax rate. Bam! A 30% tax hit would leave you with only about $700,000 of that million dollar dream because Uncle Sam is just waiting to get paid on all that income. Wake up! Utilizing a tax-deferred retirement account works best for those who are in a low tax bracket when they start accessing it. The tax sting can also be diminished by taking using retirement funds base on the IRS guidelines for minimum distribution or adhering to Stretch IRA rules. This action will be explained in chapter 9 as part of the AAA (Asset Accumulation Access) Approach.

Do you see why I recommend engaging in accounts that will provide for tax-**deferred** growth coupled with tax-**free** Distributions? Would you rather have... $1,006,000, $720,000 or $513,000? It is your choice.

But wait, those of you who are most astute will note that the original $100,000 in a tax free environment would have had to be taxed. Okay, so we had to start with roughly $135,000 to pay the tax, and have $100,000 left to invest and grow tax free. So let's subtract another $35,000 from our compounded, tax-free example. The total is now $971.000. Still, compare that with the third column where we were taxed 30% annually and end up with $513,000. Friends, compounding is significant. Tax-deferred makes an incredible impact. *Yet, it is the tax-free accumulation that is the Holy Grail!*

With this new knowledge, you are in control. You can choose to keep all of the money that your money earns, or you can give up to 50% or more to the government. You can provide a larger nest egg for your family by taking advantage of this simple principle of tax-deferral and ultimately, tax-free distributions using the RAFT Strategy.

So what is the difference between Tax-Deferred and Tax-Free? Please understand, so many people think those two terms are interchangeable and they are not.

Notice that the following chart allows for the account owner to withdraw from a tax-deferred account enough from a million dollar nest egg annually to end up $75,000 net spendable dollars every year. Notice how the account is depleted within 15 years because tax must be paid on every withdrawal:

One Million Dollars earning 7.5% interest in a 35% Tax bracket

$1,000,000	Account Value
7.50%	Rate of Return
35%	Tax Bracket
$115,385	Must Withdraw
$75,000	Net spendable $

Taxable Distributions

Age	Withdraw	7.5% ROI	Acct Value	
64	0 of 1,000,000	75,000	1,075,000	
65	115,385	71,971	1,031,587	Maintained your
66	115,385	68,715	984,917	lifestyle from 65 to 79,
67	115,385	65,215	934,747	but ended up outliving
68	115,385	61,452	880,815	your money
69	115,385	57,407	822,838	
70	115,385	53,059	760,512	
71	115,385	48,385	693,512	
72	115,385	43,360	621,487	
73	115,385	37,958	544,060	
74	115,385	32,151	460,826	$1 million gone
75	115,385	25,908	371,349	in 14.5 years
76	115,385	19,197	275,162	
77	115,385	11,983	171,761	
78	115,385	4,228	60,605	
79	**60,605**	**0**	**0**	

You've maintained your lifestyle for almost 15 years, but will outlive your income. In contrast, subtracting annual distributions of $75,000 from a tax-free account shows us quite a different picture:

Tax Free Distributions:

One Million Dollars earning 7.5% interest with 0% Tax

$1,000,000	Account Value
7.50%	Rate of Return
0%	Tax Bracket
$75,000	Must Withdraw
$75,000	Net spendable $

Tax-Free Distributions

Age	Withdraw	7.5% ROI	Acct Value
64	0 of 1,000,000	75,000	1,075,000
65	75,000	75,000	1,075,000
66	75,000	75,000	1,075,000
67	75,000	75,000	1,075,000
68	75,000	75,000	1,075,000
69	75,000	75,000	1,075,000
70	75,000	75,000	1,075,000
71	75,000	75,000	1,075,000
72	75,000	75,000	1,075,000
73	75,000	75,000	1,075,000
74	75,000	75,000	1,075,000
75	75,000	75,000	1,075,000
76	75,000	75,000	1,075,000
77	75,000	75,000	1,075,000
78	75,000	75,000	1,075,000
79	75,000	75,000	1,075,000

Pass on a legacy!

From 65 to whenever...

Once again you can see that taking tax-free distributions blows the tax-deferred option out of the water. You have effectively lived off the interest of your nest egg and can leave a million dollar legacy to your children or whoever you want.

Ask yourself, "What would I rather count on. . .Increasing taxable income, or an unencumbered nest egg, free from tax?" Some of these choices may have already been made. So, we can help you navigate your way back into the best option for you by perhaps limiting your qualified contributions to only those matched by your employer, especially if you are still under age 62, or by sharing with you how to roll out of a qualified plan into the RAFT Strategy.

Are you funding a qualified retirement plan already? If you are, or even if you're considering that one day you might; you're going to want to read carefully. I'm talking about the pros and cons of qualified retirement plans. You know them, they are namely, IRAs, 401(k)s, SEP, 403(b)s, TSPs, and 457 pension plans. And there are more. They all have these numbers and letters associated with them so they can seem confusing and mysterious at times. Yet these qualified accounts are sanctioned by the IRS and allow us to save for our future retirement tax-deferred.

I hope by now this is crystal clear to you: tax-deferred does not mean tax-free. It means tax **procrastination**. We save on taxes when we contribute because, within certain limitations, we can deduct the amount that we filter into qualified accounts from our income. Thus, we do not pay tax on contributions until we access the account years later. Sounds pretty good, right? We all like tax deductions because they translate into more immediate money in our pockets. . .and we like the feeling of having more money in our pockets right NOW.

Here's the problem:

All qualified plans are set up with strings attached.

This is a glaring flaw in the system. I look at those strings attached just like the strings on a puppet. All of us that have IRAs are the puppets and we are controlled by the Marionette, who is Uncle SAM. I don't know about you, but I am very freedom oriented. I don't do well with the whole 'strings attached' concept. I'd rather be Pinocchio -the real boy- and have some freedom with my accounts, than Pinocchio -the puppet.

So what are these strings? There are at least 5. To help you understand what they are, I want you to visualize yourself as the puppet who is dancing to the tune of qualified plans. Let's imagine for a minute that there is one string attached to each leg, one attached to each arm and one to your head. Does this mean that Uncle SAM will take an arm and a leg and he'll mess with your head? Well, I think he has already messed with your head if you're putting all your hard earned cash into one of his 'qualified' accounts.

Hold on now, don't get all ruffled here. We know your employers think they are doing you a great favor by matching your 401(k) contribution. Believe me, we are thankful and accept the gift. (I suggest you take as much as your employer will provide.) At the same time, ask yourself, "Does it make sense to fund my 401(k) beyond the employer match, when I could be placing that extra money in an account that can give me tax-free accumulation and distributions?"

The caveats when it comes to sinking money into those qualified accounts are significant. Let me explain in a way you can remember. Now visualize yourself as that puppet. . . the IRS puppet. Again, I'm talking about one of those puppets with the strings attached; controlled by a marionette. We are the puppet and the IRS is a Marionette.

String number one is attached to your head; your mind. Uncle SAM may not purposely confuse us but he sure has a way of making our minds do flip flops each year at tax time when we're deciding whether or not we ought to make our yearly contribution to an IRA. Remember that there are strict regulations governing IRS qualified retirement plans like IRA, 401ks, SEPs, and Roth IRSs. Contributions are dictated by our income because we're limited to how much we're allowed to contribute tax-deferred. So don't count on the opportunity to build your IRA quickly by making a substantial annual investment.

Your head may be thinking, "Now if I don't make enough money, there is no sense in contributing because the tax break isn't enough incentive. Even though I may deduct the contribution now, I know I will have to pay tax on 100% of the account, including the growth, when I take distributions. And if I make too much money, I am not allowed to fund my Roth IRA."

If any of these scenarios describe you, don't be concerned. There is a better alternative and it employs three important wealth building principles: Safety, Liquidity, and Rate of Return. We call it the RAFT Strategy and it utilizes a properly designed and funded EIUL (Equity Indexed Universal Life) contract with top rated Insurance companies. Companies that have been serving policyholders for decades and some have been around for over a century.

You know, people ask me all the time, "Is this safe, setting up essentially a bank account with an insurance company?" I look them straight in the eye and share with them that YES, it is actually one of the safest places you can place your hard-earned money. There are more than 2,000 life insurance companies in the U.S. and they collectively own, manage or control more assets than all banks in the world combined. They also collectively own, manage, or control more assets than all of the oil companies in the world combined.

If one company opts to close their doors, there are approximately 1999 other companies that can and will take over the policyholders contracts. By law, these companies are obligated to adhere to the parameters of each individual policy; thus, protecting these valuable assets for the policyholders.

In fact, during the Great Depression, it was the insurance companies, not the federal government, that bailed out the banking industry. Insurance companies are also required by the State in which they do business to maintain enough assets to fulfill all of their financial obligations to their policyholders. There are other safeguards in place making many insurance companies among the largest and most solvent enterprises in the world.

OK, let's get back to our IRS Puppet Strings. String number two is attached to your right leg: this time the Marionette in control is your 'old school' financial planner who does not want you to put your foot down to avoid risk and get better rates of return. The typical IRA account is 'managed' by a 'Financial Adviser' or brokerage house in the form of Mutual funds or individual stocks. Have you ever tried to get hold of your adviser to make changes? It's crazy! By the time they finally respond, the moment is gone.

Ok, let's cut the old school financial planner a break. We all know it's impossible to flawlessly gauge the stock market. In fact, as stated in the book, *Blind Faith* by Edward Winslow, less than 4% of the money managers' portfolios under management meet or beat the growth of the S&P 500. The other 96% failed to get 100% of the gains in the market.

It is no wonder that, according to the DALBAR report, we see actual gains for investors are an average of 2.57% per year, not the 7+% returns that you may hear about from an old school financial planner. Now, technically, they are correct because they are looking at *average* returns. They did not consider that per cent gains on a lower base, following a loss, does not equal the same gain as it would on the original principal, prior to the loss. You see COMPOUND returns are not the same as AVERAGE RETURNS. That is why the principle of locking in the gains as your new principal every year and protecting your account against losses is so critically important to increasing your nest egg.

Look at is this way:

If you had $100 in an investment and it lost 50%, your investment would have to gain back 100% on that lower base to earn its way back to its original principal. We will focus most on the lock-in and reset principle in the next chapter as we discuss exactly how the RAFT Strategy works.

For now, just remember that the RAFT Strategy has a Principal Guarantee, so your account will experience the upside of the market and the gains are locked in. When there is a downturn, your account sits it out and remains steady until the market increases again, at which time, your account increases as well and your gains are automatically locked in as principal. That is called *Safety* while still getting a good *Rate of Return*.

Securing your safety of principal is a primary value for us at Freedom Financial. Don't take this wrong, but your old school adviser really doesn't care. Why should they? They get paid coming and going. They get a kick-back every time your money is traded. That is why I say that old school adviser may be acting a marionette. With that string of risk attached to your right foot, your progress and security are in jeopardy. Do not let it happen. You need to put your foot down and get rid of that string of *Risk*.

How are we doing with our strings attached? Let's look at string number 3: The *Lack of Liquidity* string attached to your right hand.

Ask yourself, "What happens if I want to use my money prior to age 59 ½?" Well, there is a penalty for early withdrawal. You got it; a 10% penalty in addition to income tax on any amount that you withdraw. "So that means I don't really have 100% access to my money, right?" You are correct. There is a string attached in a big way! It's attached to your right hand and our marionette, Uncle SAM, won't let that hand reach into your own pocket to use your own money, without a penalty. That's called *Lack of Liquidity*.

Qualified plans don't pass one of the basic criteria for wise money management. Wealthy people have access to their money when the want it. *The wealthy have liquidity.* When you understand how the RAFT Strategy can work for you, it may even make sense to take an early withdrawal from your IRA, pay the penalty and the tax, and transfer your money into something safe and secure; a program that provides compounding tax-free growth.

We've already discussed the IRS string of confusion attached to your head, the Old School Financial adviser's string of risk attached to your right foot and Uncle SAM's string of non-liquidity preventing your right arm from reaching your own pocket. Are you feeling tied up yet? Now we're going to showcase the strings on the left side of your puppet investment body. They have to do with our age and the transfer of our wealth at death, which I call 'Lights Out'.

The fourth IRS string attached to your qualified account is connected to your left foot. You may be thinking, "Hey, by age 70 and ½ I'll have one foot in the grave." But the IRS doesn't care about that. They will get your tax, dead or alive. The truth is that people are living longer these days, and statistically, if you have already made it to age 65, plan to live to 85 years old, give or take a few years depending on your gender and whether or not you are married. (Believe it or not, married couples live 3-4 years longer, on average than do singles.)

You'll need to plan for and project your income stream to last into your 90s. Guess what? You may want to stretch your retirement funds out a bit. But what happens if you don't start withdrawing from your account at age 70 ½? You know the answer. If you don't start withdrawing from your qualified account at age 70 ½, the government is going to slam you with a 50% penalty. You see, you are an investment for the government. They aren't stupid. Your retirement account is Uncle SAM's investment; He has a permanent tax lien on your qualified account, and He wants His return. The money that you contributed will have compounded and guess what? Its harvest time for Uncle Sam!

Uncle Sam gets **all** the income tax on a much larger amount than the contribution because you deferred payment of your income taxes. So you see, if you do not start tapping into that IRA, Uncle SAM doesn't get His ROI (Return On Investment) and you get clobbered with a 50% penalty. . .now That is hefty. Your accountant never put it to you like that when you saved a few bucks by deferring your taxes, years ago. You will ultimately pay many times more tax on the qualified account that has been growing over years, than if you would have bit the bullet way back then, paid your tax, and let your account accumulate tax-free, instead of tax-deferred.

And finally, the government is going to get their tax whether you are dead or alive. Hence, string attached # 5. The 5th and final IRS puppet string is attached to your left hand; the generous one; the one that is constantly giving and sharing your success with family members. And when you pass on, Uncle SAM is going to do some reaching of his own - right into the pockets of your heirs. Someone has got to pay that tax and if you didn't take care of it while you were living, your beneficiaries will have to take care of it once you are gone.

Yes, that is right. Your transference of wealth in the form of a qualified retirement plan is fully taxed, leaving your beneficiaries with much less, than had you engaged in the tax-free strategy to begin with. So, drawback #5 is that even once you are gone, if you still have a balance in that qualified account, your beneficiaries are relegated to paying State and Federal tax, based on their current tax bracket.

Why would you want that to happen, when you can prevent it? Folks, you can use the *Triple Crown of Safe Investing* to cut the strings that are attached to your financial future. By implementing a properly designed RAFT Strategy account you can eliminate all five issues we just discussed. Deposit amounts that make a difference in your life. Take already taxed money at today's low rates and put it to work for you. Get the money from any one or a combination of sources: savings, CD's, money markets, stocks, your bank account, your monthly income, or even your mattress.

Mathematically, cashing in and taking the 10% penalty now on your IRA may work out better for you than paying income tax on 100% of the account during your retirement. Talk to the Strategic Wealth Coach that gave you this book, or register to find an SWC through our website: www.RAFTstrategy.com. It's all about maximizing your cash flow and getting tax-free distributions and an illustration from a trained and skilled adviser, who can show you how and what is available to you at any given time.

Under the IRS Code, you are able to make tax deferred contributions to a qualified tax-deferred account, let it grow tax-deferred and pay tax on every penny once you access it. Or, according to your income, you may be able to use after tax money to set up a Roth IRA that will accumulate tax free and you can access it tax free after age 59 ½. You choose. Of course, accessing your money without having to pay any more tax is ideal.

We believe Roth IRAs are preferable to traditional IRAs because of the tax-free distribution provision; yet Roth IRAs are very limited. As of the writing of this book, single Americans are only allowed to fully fund a Roth IRA provided they made an AGI (Adjusted Gross Income) of under $112,000. Anyone making $112,000 to $127,000 can still participate on a limited basis, and those earning over $127,000 are not allowed to contribute at all. Also; the annual contribution to a Roth IRA for singles under age 50 is limited to only $5000. (Starting last year, in 2012, these contributions increase limits are indexed to inflation.) If you are married filing separately and you make over $10,000, you are not allowed to contribute, married couples can only partially contribute, provided they earn less than $188,000 and fully participate with a joint income of less than $178,000. . .the list of caveats goes on and on. (See the chart at the end of this Chapter.)

Roth IRAs are a good idea, but it is tough to accumulate much unless you engage in a conversion from your traditional IRA. If the Roth conversion option is exercised, all the tax has to be paid at once; which isn't pretty. You know what kind of major hole that can make in your nest egg.

The bottom line is: You have a choice. You can cut those puppet strings. You don't have to relegate yourself to paying taxes on all of your retirement accounts. You can decide how much of your money you want to set aside in qualified plans and how much you want to preserve in a tax-free environment. Not everybody can qualify for the RAFT. And it may or may not work for you, depending on your health and *time horizon* (perceived years left in your lifetime). It doesn't necessarily work for everyone. I typically suggest the strategy for those between 20 and 65 years old who have enough assets to live on, apart from what they want to shift into the RAFT or other retirement vehicles.

We've shared with you some of the characteristics of the RAFT Strategy. In the next chapter you'll see how a Strategic Wealth Coach can set it up properly for you and teach you how to properly take tax-free distributions. Tell me; where else are you going to get safety, liquidity, and generous tax-free compounding? We want you to be able to contribute as much as you can to a tax-free account. We want you to have access to your money when you need it, without a 10% penalty. We want you to enjoy tax-free accumulation, compounded growth and a **Retirement Account Free of Tax.**

2013 Traditional & Roth IRA Contribution Limits

Traditional & Roth IRA Contributions and Catch Up Provisions		
Plan Name	Standard Limit	Catch-up Limit (Age 50 and older)
Traditional	$5,500	$6,500
Roth*	$5,500	$6,500

Modified AGI Limits:
2013
Single: $112,000 - $127,000
Married Filing Jointly: $178,000 - 188,000
2013 Traditional & Roth IRA Contribution Deadline is 4/15/2014

Provided you are still in search of a Strategic Wealth Coach, contact us through our website: www.RAFTstrategy.com and we will direct you to a licensed, trained and qualified SWC in your area. The SWC can provide an illustration, based on your needs; according to your age, gender, health status, and years until retirement. The illustration will show how the RAFT Strategy can work for you and your family.

Chapter 5

First Jewel of the
Triple Crown Solution:

The RAFT Strategy

**(Properly designed and funded Equity Indexed
Universal Life insurance contract)**

At HERO'S Talk Radio, Freedom Financial Network, we often refer to our investment philosophy as the *Triple Crown Solution* because we showcase three distinct, safe investing secrets that provide guaranteed protection and growth for retirement accounts.

As we unveil the mystery of the RAFT Strategy to our listeners, we often hear, "This sounds way too good to be true." Well, I can see why that comment surfaces time and again, because where else can we get an average compounded growth rate of over 8%, tax-free? Since it may seem inconceivable to you, I will share with you how the RAFT Strategy came to be, and why it works better today than ever before. To begin, let's take a quick tour through the history of insurance so you will understand how the RAFT Strategy evolved into its present form.

Term Insurance
(Temporary Life Insurance)

We all know about Term Life insurance. Some of the earliest term life insurance started in 1759 by the Presbyterian Ministers Fund to provide for the wife and kids in the farmhouse, should the husband, out in the field meet with an untimely end. In those days, there was no auto-pay or electronic transfer. Every month the insurance agent had to stop by the house of each policyholder to collect the premium. The premium paid the face amount of the policy in place and just like Term insurance today, the younger and healthier the policyholder, the less the coverage would cost.

Term Insurance is named such because the contract is set up for a certain number of years until it expires. For example, one can purchase a policy for ten, twenty or even thirty years, depending on the terms of the contract. Term insurance is used strictly to provide a death benefit. The death benefit is determined by the age, gender and health of the policy holder. No cash value accrues within the account as it can in a Whole Life or Indexed Life Policy. There is a definite purpose for Term insurance when an individual's main concern is to protect the beneficiaries should the policyholder pass away. The policy is purchased according to the length of time it will remain in force before recalculating the cost.

Term policies are owned for a specific period of time (or Term), typically when the owner has the greatest need to provide for others. The biggest draw to Term is the cost. Term life insurance is inexpensive when the insured is young and increases in cost as the insured ages. Usually owners keep the insurance long enough to fulfill a specific need, such as the payoff of a home mortgage, care for young children, or the replacement of family income in case of death.

The fact is that only about 3% of Term Policies ever pay to a beneficiary because generally, each time a term policy expires, the premium dramatically increases. Most policyholders consider dropping the term policy when they see the astronomical increase in premium costs. A typical policyholder will then weigh the pros and cons of having the coverage at the increased rate (sometimes 10 times the original price!) just to keep it going. Usually the answer is, "It's just not worth the price".

Also, the policyholder may not pass the physical health exam at the time of renewal because their health condition has changed from the time they began the original term policy. They may no longer be an acceptable risk for the insurance company, so the company has the option to drop them as a policyholder.

Paying into Term Policy is much like renting or leasing a home. The owner pays for it as long as they think it is needed. Whereas Permanent Life insurance is like buying a home, and building equity in that home as it is paid for throughout the years. Enough said about Term insurance. Now let's focus on policies that can provide Living Benefits in addition to Death Benefits.

Whole Life
(Permanent Life Insurance)

Around 1860, about 100 years after Term Insurance became available, Whole Life Insurance was created. This gave birth to the investment side of life insurance. A whole life insurance contract builds equity for the policyholder. A portion of the premium (funds paid into the account) is used to pay for the insurance, and the rest is placed in a cash accumulation account. The policy can be paid with a set amount or it can increase from year to year, according to the owner's preference.

Why would someone want to increase premiums as they age? Because the cost of insurance goes up as we age, so once the insurance is covered, any extra cash will accumulate and build interest according to the parameters of the policy. Bottom line is the policy has both insurance, and an investment component. The insurance component pays a stated amount upon death of the insured. The investment component accumulates cash value which the policyholder can withdraw tax-deferred. They can also borrow against the face amount, tax-free. The following illustration shows how the cash value increases as the face value decreases in a standard Whole Life policy:

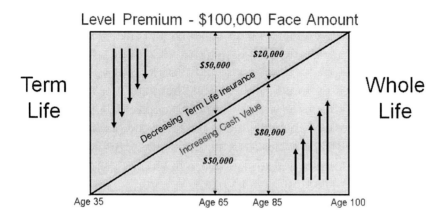

Level Premium - $100,000 Face Amount

Whole Life has gone through a metamorphosis over the past 150 years. The efficacy of the investment side of life has come into question numerous times as interest rates and the economy have shifted over the years. In fact, the high inflation rates and high interest rates that developed during the Jimmy Carter years and into the 1980s brought the Whole Life investment idea to its knees because insurance companies' dividends didn't even come close to meeting current interest rates of the time.

Remember when you (or your parents) could go down to the local bank and get a CD that would pay 12-15% interest? Do you remember, also, that home mortgage rates were 16-18%? Well, whole life policy holders were not about to keep their money tied up in a life policy yielding 2% when they could buy a cheaper term policy and invest the balance in other, more productive, investment vehicles. "Buy Term, invest the rest," became the mantra with good reason and many today believe nothing has changed. Yet, *everything* has changed. Please bear with me for a few more descriptions and you will see why the RAFT Strategy has risen above all other forms of insurance to create safety, liquidity, a great rate of return, and tax-free distributions.

Universal Life Insurance

Whereas Whole life insurance caters to long-term goals by offering consumers consistent premiums and guaranteed cash value accumulation, Universal life insurance gives consumers flexibility in the premium payments, death benefits, and the savings element of their policy. For decades, Universal Life (UL) and Variable (VUL) have existed with a number of features and options: Single Premium, Fixed Premium, and Flexible Premium. The movement in the cash value fluctuates with the allocation options. A policy owner will enjoy increased interest credits based on the parameters of the policy. Typically the owner has the ability to periodically change investment strategies within the cash account, yet may not be able to lock-in the gains from year to year.

Policyholders loved the flexibility of UL and VUL policies which were so popular in the 80s and 90s when the equity markets seemed to be ever trending upwards. The caveat being that what goes up often comes down, and these policies did not contain a feature to lock in gains from year to year. The policies, therefore, contained an element of risk, unless the fixed allocation was used.

There are so many variations in policies that it is imperative to seek the advice of a licensed professional who can base the selection of a policy on your particular needs. So in summary, we have the economy of Term, the permanence security of Whole Life, the flexibility of Universal Life, and the opportunity of Variable Universal, but we didn't have all of those features wrapped up into a neat package until Equity Indexed Universal Life (EIUL) was developed in the late 1990s. Now you'll see why it was worth the wait.

Equity Indexed Universal Life

The magic of risk free growth exists in permanent EIUL. As the new kid on the block, the EIUL was developed in the late 1990s, and the first policy was introduced in 1997. To explain the magic of how we use EIUL policies to create the RAFT, which is a properly designed, funded and accessed EIUL, I'm going to give you the Top Ten best reasons for engaging in the RAFT Strategy.

The RAFT strategy, just like a life raft, serves to buoy you up in the midst of the troubling waters of the economy, increasing taxes, and a volatile stock market. It serves to protect your accounts against the flood of government stupidity, and the currents of inflation.

Utilizing this safe account strategy, you won't lose a dime due to external forces that you have no control over. Whether it's actual tsunamis or geographical earthquakes, or its financial tsunamis or political tremors; those crazy things that cause the real estate and stock market (or should I say *SHOCK* market) to get sucked down into a proverbial whirlpool, will not sink your Life*RAFT*.

So, ala David Letterman style, here we go. . . The Top Ten reasons to engage in the RAFT Strategy are:

#10. . .There is no age requirement to begin the account or to access funds. In fact, we have clients who have started funding the RAFT Strategy for their children. We have helped young couples in their 20s and grandparents alike to open the policy with a mind towards funding their future children's or grandchildren's college education. AND, we utilize the IRS guidelines 1035 exchange provision which allows for an insurance policy to transfer from one insurance company to another insurance company without tax consequences. We have helped numerous retirees to work with the RAFT to create a more safe and solid, **tax-free** future for themselves and to provide a legacy for their beneficiaries.

#9. . .Asset Protection: We live in a litigious society, where when people get miffed about things, sometimes they want to get even, get revenge, get a free ride, or maybe they just want to be indemnified; made whole after an unfortunate event. Well in most states, money housed within the RAFT strategy is protected from lawsuits of any kind. This is especially attractive to business owners, physicians, and other professionals who are always on the lookout to protect their hard earned assets, which have taken years to grow. They can breathe a sigh of relief knowing that their nest egg is protected from the unscrupulous actions of those who view our civil justice system as their free ride to unearned wealth.

#8. . .Liquidity: Having access to our own money, when we need it and when we want it! Isn't it comforting to know that we don't have to wait until we are 59 ½ to use our own retirement funds without incurring a 10% tax penalty? Isn't it great that we don't

HAVE to extract the money when we're 70 ½ to avoid a 50% tax penalty? Such is not true of those tax-deferred, or shall I say *'tax-procrastination'* qualified plans. You've heard of them, and you may even own one or two. They are the IRAs, 401(k)s, 457 Plans, TSPs, 403(b)s and so forth.

Still, **even though** we recommend the RAFT Strategy for Tax-Free Retirement, **we do suggest** our clients patiently allow it to grow and compound for the future, for at least 10 years. In fact, as an owner of the RAFT Account, I **CAN** access my money, should I need it, without incurring a penalty or tax consequence, even before I'm 59 ½. AND, I'm not forced to access it at 70 ½ to avoid a penalty. Those qualified plans do have the gotchas. Wouldn't you like to know that you can have access to your money whenever you need it, without penalty or incurring heavy interest charges? Well *liquidity* is one of the best features of the RAFT Strategy.

#7. . .Rate of Return: Historically, over the past 30 years, and even over the past 10 years, our RAFT Strategy has yielded an average of 8-9% RoR, based on the **gains** of the equity markets. The account can yield up to 16% depending on which insurance company is used.

Did you hear me? I'm not talking about a secured 1 or 2% growth like in a money market or CD. I'm talking about up to 16% growth compounded annually and tax-free. Since the account experiences no losses during market downturns, it yields only positive returns, so the **average** 8-9% RoR is the **REAL** rate of return.

Additionally, once we have started funding the RAFT Strategy, the owner of the account has a choice every year on the anniversary date (the day in the year on which the account began) to either keep the account tied to the growth of the equity markets, or to receive a fixed amount. Now this is remarkable because I'm guessing you would be hard pressed to find a higher fixed rate anywhere.

Are you ready for this? As of 2013, the current **fixed** rate of return is 4.9%. That percentage is subject to change, and yet over the past 4 years that we have been talking about the RAFT Strategy on the radio, the fixed rate offered by various insurance companies has been between 4.5 to 5.3%, even with the weird volatility of the Market.

Of course, nobody has a crystal ball, but if you did, and you thought the Market was going to be flat or take a dive in the coming year, wouldn't you like to know that you could opt to have your RAFT allocated to a fixed rate of almost 5%, instead of experiencing no gain? I would, and I do.

In fact, I believe we are likely to see more of the same in the Market before we see a steady upturn. I hope I'm wrong, but when I do annual reviews with our clients, I make sure they know they have an option to bow out of the Market for a year and still get a pretty nice rate of return. I mean, 4.9% is far superior; about 3-4 times what money markets and CDs are offering. As of May 2013, CDs are earning a paltry 75-1.75% depending on the term. How would you like to have a guaranteed 4.9% increase LOCKED into your retirement account this year? As long as the RAFT Strategy is set up properly and funded correctly, those increases inside of the EIUL contract can be accessed tax-free and transferred tax-free as well! So our #7 reason to engage in the RAFT Strategy is the great Rate of Return.

#6. . . In my opinion, the most magical ingredient of the RAFT Strategy is its annual *Lock-in and Re-set* provision. This dynamic feature enables the RAFT account holder to capture the positive market return every year and lock it into the principal, creating a new, higher principal amount, which can only grow from there, as long as it continues to be funded properly.

Let's discuss this: So, for example, if a $100,000 account experienced a 10% gain one year, the new principal amount would be locked in at $110,000. Then, should the Market fall 10% the next year, the RAFT policy would not lose a penny due to the Market decline; whereas, a traditional brokerage account would have lost the 10%, taking the new balance **backwards** to $99,000. Do you want $99,000 or $110,000 after your two year investment? It's your choice.

Now let's say the Market gains 5% the 3rd year. Well, the brokerage account would get back up to $103,950, but the RAFT account would then be over 115,500 because it started from a higher base. You see, when 33% is lost in an investment, it takes a 50% gain just to get back to the original principal balance. Don't be duped by the broker that says, "Our average return is 7%," or whatever. Remember, **average rates of return** become the **real rate of return ONLY** when the gains are locked in, and there is **never a loss**.

Keep in mind, this is all about protecting your assets and having access to your money **tax-free** at the same time. So next time we would see an increase in the Markets to which your account is linked, your principal would bump up as far as the cap, which right now, in 2013, is as much as 16 %. Don't you think it is time to get your hands on this information? This may be the answer for you and your family, like it was for me. We have planned RAFT accounts for each of our 7 children and now we are looking at getting RAFTs funded for the grandkids.

Learn how this is done by requesting an illustration through our website: www.RAFTstrategy.com. We can educate you. You can't set up the RAFT by yourself. It does require a licensed Strategic Wealth Coach to process the request according to IRS guidelines. And remember, each of the SWCs is independent. They are not obligated to any particular company and they are only compensated by the companies once they have opened up a new RAFT within that company. They are free to evaluate and choose the best financial fit for their clients.

You know, I crunched some numbers for a 46 year old to find out what the impact of waiting even a month to start employing the RAFT Strategy would be. I found out that for every year she waited to begin, she was losing $5,000 off of her annual distributions once she hit 65 years old. That is an average loss of $4-500/month just because she didn't pay attention and make it a priority to start the RAFT as soon as she could. Time is money folks. Contact us so one of our SWCs can get your complimentary illustration to you as soon as possible.

Why wait to get this information? It's free. In fact it's better than free. Our affiliate coaches don't even charge for their expertise because they are licensed in your area and specially trained on how to setup the RAFT properly; utilizing an appropriate EIUL contract with a top rated insurance company. They have the responsibility to get an illustration on how the RAFT Strategy may work for you into your hands. You can learn how to get on the right side of taxes and have all kinds of other great benefits as well by requesting the complimentary personalized illustration now.

How do you like the TOP 10 reasons for employing the RAFT strategy, so far? We've already talked about: No age requirement, Asset Protection, Liquidity, Rate of Return, and the Interest Credit Lock-in and Reset of the Index provision. But hang onto your hats folks, there's more.

Five down, five to go.

#5. . .Principal Guarantees: This is the magic bullet of the RAFT Strategy. Remember that average returns are not the same as compound returns unless you never experience losses. The RAFT Strategy uses an Equity Indexed Universal Life Policy that is linked to the indexes and insures your account against losses.

For example, if the S&P 500 or the NASDAQ goes down that year, your account balance remains level, it does not drop. Your RAFT receives 0% and maintains principal. In this sense, *Zero is our Hero*. Your account only goes up with the indexes, not down; **EVER.** Think about it. You have a choice. You can keep your money in a risky position or you can have your principal guaranteed with the RAFT Strategy. The choice is yours to move your money into a safe place and still get a great RoR, or not. To quote the iconic Nike ad, I'd say, "Just do it."

Below is a chart of the real S&P number compared to the RAFT increases during the famous 'lost decade' 2000 through 2010, which, in my words, has now turned into the 'Dirty Dozen', encompassing 2011 -2012. Note the compounded rate of return on each side of the chart. In the worst period since the great Depression, the increases in the RAFT were over 100% (minus cost of insurance, loads and fees) whereas the S&P had a negative 1% compounded RoR, showing the compounded effect of -1.07 average RoR. This resulted in a 9 % loss from 2000 through 2011. The returns for 2012 thankfully, once again, brought the average nest egg back to where it was at the end of 1999 and 2007.

The Market volatility of the past 12 years is one reason so many people are frustrated with the equity markets and are questioning placing their hard-earned nest eggs into them. Without having a Principal Guarantee, who knows how long the up and down madness could last. These numbers on the next chart may look very familiar to you. Do you see a reflection of the 'Dirty Dozen' in your 401(k), IRA or personal stock accounts in the following chart?

S&P 500 vs. RAFT Strategy

Year	S&P 500	$100,000	RAFT (16%Cap)	$100,000
2000	-10.14%	$89,860.00	0.95%	$100,950
2001	-13.04%	$78,142.26	0.00%	$100,950
2002	-23.37%	$59,880.41	0.00%	$100,950
2003	26.38%	$75,676.86	16.00%	$117,102
2004	8.99%	$82,480.21	5.70%	$123,776.81
2005	3.00%	$84,954.62	5.23%	$130,250.34
2006	13.62%	$96,525.44	11.94%	$145,802.23
2007	3.53%	$99,932.79	5.77%	$154,215.02
2008	-34.12%	$65,835.72	0.00%	$154,215.02
2009	23.50%	$81,307.11	15.42%	$177,994.98
2010	12.80%	$91,714.42	7.51%	$191,362.40
2011	-.43%	$91,320.05	0.72%	$192,740.21
2012	7.99%	**$98,616.52**	8.24%	**$208,622.00**
Avg.	Compounding	**-0.107%**	Tax Free	**6.45%**

Note: The RAFT Strategy returns are based on the performance of EIUL contracts and show the increase in the cash value side of the account. In adherence to IRS guidelines, proper and strategic access to the cash value is imperative. We often say, here at Freedom Financial, "There are three ways to get cash out of a life insurance policy; the smart way, the dumb way, and the sad way." We will discuss these three methods to access money from the RAFT Strategy in the following chapter, but here is a quick peek:

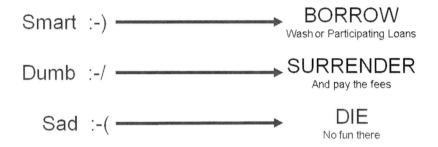

Smart :-) ⟶ BORROW
Wash or Participating Loans

Dumb :-/ ⟶ SURRENDER
And pay the fees

Sad :-(⟶ DIE
No fun there

Now back to our top 10:

#4. . .Survivor Benefit: Should something happen to you, like terminal illness, disability, or death, your RAFT account blossoms in value and provides comfort and security for yourself and your loved ones. That protection has been a huge blessing in lives of many of our client. I never want to worry or wonder what would happen to my family if something drastic happened to me. I know that my family can experience the full value of my hard earned assets whether I am with them or not because I took a small amount of time out of my busy schedule to set up my own RAFT Strategy. Even though taking the death benefit is the *sad* way to get money out of my RAFT; knowing my family is financially secure as long as I live and beyond gives me comfort.

#3. . .Tax-Deferred Growth: The best way to cover this is by illustrating a familiar analogy. As we discussed in Chapter 4, if you had a dollar in an investment and that investment doubled tax-deferred every year for 20 years, at the end of 20 years, you would have over 1 million dollars.

Yet, if you had that same dollar and again it doubled every year and you had to pay just 15% tax, as earned, annually, (akin to Capital Gain Tax) you would end up with just over $220,000. Taking it a step further, that same dollar doubled every year. . .and taxed at 30% annually would yield a little over $40,000. So, does tax-deferral make a difference? You bet it does! Tax-deferred growth is employing the miracle of Compound Interest. . . as Albert Einstein reportedly put it, "Compound interest is the 8th wonder of the world." Tax-deferral is compliments of the IRS. Isn't it time to make Uncle Sam your partner, not your foe!?!

#2. . .Tax-Free Access: Even better than tax-deferred, the RAFT Strategy has built in IRS approved provisions that enable tax-free access to the money in your account. According to 72e and 7702 of the IRS code, plus the Tax relief acts from the 1980s, TEFRA, DEFRA and TAMRA, your account value can be accessed tax-free by borrowing against the death benefit. As an example, if you have an EIUL with a death benefit of $500,000, and while you are living you borrow out $450,000, at 'lights out' the insurance company would understand that $450,000 of the Death Benefit was already paid out. The insurance company would subtract the total borrowed from the death benefit, leaving the remaining $50,000 to your beneficiaries, tax-free.

The secret is: *When the owner of the EIUL policy borrows from the Death Benefit, that loan comes out of the policy tax-free!* For example let's say you borrowed interest-free from your EIUL $50,000 to live on for your retirement. Or, maybe you needed it to pay for a daughter's wedding or a grandchild's tuition, you only have to take $50,000 out of the account to be able to spend $50,000. You don't have to extract 75,000 in order to pay the 33% tax and then have only $50,000 to spend. Your nest egg may last 40% to 50% longer because you are able to extract and use that money tax-free.

And the **#1 of the Top Ten** reasons for employing the RAFT strategy is. . .Safety:

We're talking about a properly designed, and I stress *properly designed*, IRS approved contract with solid, AA and AAA life insurance repositories. The insurance companies we use to set up the RAFT accounts have been thriving for decades and some for over 100 years. We recommend some of the largest financial institutions in the world. These companies completely adhere to the IRS guidelines and are some of the safest places in the world to keep your money.

Another word about safety. . . .

Remember that famous quote that has been attributed to Will Rogers, "I'm more concerned with the return **OF** my money than the return **ON** my money." Isn't that so true? I'm a mother and a grandma and I just want us all to be happy and secure and know that our future is bright. It gives me POM POM - Peace of Mind because I have Plenty of Money. That is why the strategies we recommend on HERO'S Talk Radio are risk-free, yet still have great upside growth potential.

So there you have it, the Top 10 reasons to engage in the Retirement Approach Free of Tax, otherwise known as the RAFT Strategy. Again, they are:

1. Safety - giving you POM POM, Plenty of Money = Peace of Mind
2. Tax-Free Access - enabling your money to last longer
3. Tax-Deferred Growth - compounding your nest egg
4. Survivor Benefit - protection for those you love
5. Principal Guarantees - Zero is our Hero
6. Annual Lock-in of Gains - reset of the principal includes gains
7. Great Rate of Return – tax-deferred and tax-free
8. Liquidity - having access to your money when you want it
9. Asset Protection - both of principal and against law suits
10. No Age Requirement - penalty free withdrawals

There are more advantages, yet these are the most vivid. Ask yourself; are you ready to find out how to make Uncle Sam your partner in retirement, instead of your adversary? Are you ready to get started? It is easy to learn how by registering at our website: www.RAFTstrategy.com. We will assign an SWC in your area to contact you and provide you an illustration based on your situation.

Chapter 6

Living Benefits of the RAFT in Action

L et's talk about Tax - How can the RAFT Strategy mitigate my tax burden? Does this mean I can get away without paying any tax on my retirement approach? How does this work according to IRS regulations?

Tax Treatment of Life Insurance

Before I say anything here, know that I am not a CPA and I am not writing this book with the intent of giving tax advice. I leave that up to the accountants. My goal here is to provide education based on IRS guidelines, of how life insurance can be used to gain tax-free access to our nest egg. Now let me stress that the cash within a properly designed and funded life insurance policy can be accessed free of tax while the insured is still living, provided the cash account has accumulated enough to withdraw or borrow without lapsing the policy. The death benefit is tax-free as well, or course. Before I show you the Smart way to get your money out of a permanent life insurance policy, let's talk about the dumb way to access the money.

Remember these keys:

o The cash within an insurance policy grows tax-deferred.
o Insurance is taxed FIFO (first in, first out).

o   As a result, withdrawing from a life policy may result in a tax consequence.

o   Surrendering a life policy may trigger a tax liability on the increases.

o   And using life insurance as a Modified Endowment contract may also result in taxable liability.

Now that was confusing. Laurett just said that I can withdraw money from my whole life policy tax-deferred. . .which means that I may have to pay tax on that when I withdraw. Correct? Yes, although the basis placed into a permanent life policy is money on which tax has already been paid, so tax would not be paid again on that amount. Increases from dividends and interest are tax-deferred, so when the money is withdrawn or if the policy is surrendered, all increase is taxed FIFO unless it is a MEC (Modified Endowment Contract) which is taxed LIFO (last in, first out). LIFO means that the IRS requires the policy owner to withdraw taxable gains and pay the tax before withdrawing the non-taxable basis.

The IRS governs Modified Endowments Contracts through the Technical and Miscellaneous Revenue Act of 1988 (TAMRA) in response to single-premium life insurance policies being used as tax shelters. TAMRA established the 7-Pay Test, which stipulates that the full premium on a permanent life insurance policy must be paid within seven years of the issue date. If premiums paid to the contract exceed the premium amount stipulated, the contract fails the 7-Pay Test and is reclassified as a Modified Endowment Contract, making the interest earned within the policy taxable.

Although MECs can be a fine savings and investment vehicle and we do recommend such under certain circumstances, the purpose of this book is to educate the reader about how to create tax-free distributions, according to IRS guidelines, using a properly designed, funded and accessed EIUL.

Suffice it to say, there are complex rules and exceptions that govern the taxation of insurance products. Surrendering your life insurance policy or taking a cash withdrawal or loan from your policy each has its own set of rules and regulations, as does the taxation of the death proceeds. Because of this complexity, you'll want to work with a tax specialist who will explain how the tax code affects your policy.

Understanding the importance of life insurance is one thing. Understanding the tax rules is quite another. As insurance products have evolved and become more sophisticated, the line separating insurance vehicles from investment vehicles has grown blurry. To differentiate between the two, a mix of complex rules and exceptions now governs the taxation of insurance products. If you have neither the time nor the inclination to decipher the IRS regulations, here are some life insurance tax tips and background information to help you make sense of it all.

1) Life insurance contracts must meet IRS requirements. For federal income tax purposes, an insurance contract cannot be considered a life insurance contract—and qualify for favorable tax treatment—unless it meets state law requirements and satisfies the IRS's statutory definitions of what is or is not a life insurance policy.

The IRS considers the type of policy, date of issue, amount of the death benefit, and premiums paid. The IRS definitions are essentially tests to ensure that an insurance policy isn't really an investment vehicle. In order to ensure tax-free distributions, the insurance company must comply with these rules and enforce the provisions.

2) Keep in mind that insurance premiums cannot be deducted on your federal income tax return. Because life insurance is considered a personal expense, the owner cannot deduct the premiums paid for the coverage.

3) Employer-paid life insurance may have a tax cost. The premium cost for the first $50,000 of life insurance coverage provided under an employer-provided group term life insurance plan does not have to be reported as income and is not taxed to you. However, amounts in excess of $50,000 paid for by your employer will trigger a taxable income for the "economic value" of the coverage provided to you.

This is one reason why many feel it is important to have a personal insurance policy, even though one is provided by their employer. Not to mention that their employer may not always be their employer and there may not be a provision to retain the insurance once severed from said employment.

4) Determine whether your premiums were paid with pretax or after-tax dollars. The taxation of life insurance proceeds depends on several factors, including whether you paid your insurance premiums with pre-tax or after-tax dollars. If you buy a life insurance policy on your own or through your employer, your premiums are probably paid with after-tax dollars. Different rules may apply if your company offers the option to purchase life insurance through a qualified retirement plan and you make pre-tax contributions.

Although pre-tax contributions offer certain income tax advantages, one tradeoff is that you'll be required to pay a small tax on the economic value of the 'pure life insurance' within the policy (i.e., the difference between the cash value and the death benefit) each year. Also, at death, the amount of the policy cash value that is paid as part of the death benefit is taxable income. These days, however, not many companies offer their employees the option to purchase life insurance through their qualified retirement plan.

5) Your life insurance beneficiary probably won't have to pay income tax on death benefit received. Whoever receives the death benefit from your insurance policy usually does not have to pay Federal or State income tax on those proceeds. So, if you die owning a life insurance policy with a $500,000 death benefit, your beneficiary under the policy will likely not have to pay income tax on the receipt of the $500,000. This is generally true regardless of whether you paid all of the premiums yourself, or whether your employer subsidized part or all of the premiums under a group term insurance plan.

Different income tax rules may apply if the death benefit is paid in installments instead of as a lump sum. The interest portion (if any) of each installment is generally treated as taxable to the beneficiary at ordinary income rates, while the principal portion is tax free.

In some cases, insurance proceeds may be included in your taxable estate. If you hold any incidents of ownership in an insurance policy at the time of your death, the proceeds from that insurance policy will be included in your taxable estate. Incidents of ownership include the right to change the beneficiary, the right to take out policy loans, and the right to surrender the policy for cash. Furthermore, if you gift away an insurance policy within three years of your death, then the proceeds from that policy will be pulled back into your taxable estate. To avoid having the policy included in your taxable estate, someone other than you (e.g., a beneficiary or a trust) should be the owner.

Note: If the owner, the insured, and the beneficiary are three different people, the payment of death benefit proceeds from a life insurance policy to the beneficiary may result in an unintended taxable gift from the owner to the beneficiary. So, be careful to have a professional set up your RAFT using IRS and insurance company guidelines. It takes special software to determine to proper ratio of insurance benefit or face amount and the cash value that grows within the account. That is why an SWC can provide an illustration especially for you, according to your needs, totally free of charge by registering at our website: www.RAFTstrategy.com

Now MORE tax stuff. . .

6) If your policy has a cash value component, that part will accumulate tax-deferred. Unlike Term life insurance policies, some life insurance policies (e.g., permanent life) have a cash value component. As the cash value grows, you may ultimately have more money in cash value than you paid in premiums. Generally, you are allowed to defer income taxes on those gains as long as you don't sell, withdraw from, or surrender the policy. If you do sell, surrender, or withdraw from the policy, the difference between what you get back and what you paid in is taxed as ordinary income. That is where the Smart way of accessing the money comes in. We will teach you about Wash (or Zero spread) and participating loans, which enable you to borrow your money out of your account tax-free, without paying interest.

7) You usually aren't taxed on dividends paid. Some policies, known as participating policies; pay dividends. An insurance dividend is the amount of your premium that is paid back to you if your insurance company achieves lower mortality and expense costs than it expected. Dividends are paid out of the insurer's surplus earnings for the year. Regardless of whether you take them in cash, keep them on deposit with the insurer, or buy additional life insurance within

the policy, they are considered a return of premiums. As long as you don't get back more than you paid in, you are merely recouping your costs, and no tax is due. However, if you leave these dividends on deposit with your insurance company and they earn interest, the interest you receive should be included as taxable interest income.

8) Watch out for cash withdrawals in excess of basis—they're taxable. That is why we suggest *borrowing* your money out instead of taking withdrawals.

If you withdraw cash from a cash value life insurance policy, the amount of withdrawals up to your basis in the policy will be tax free. Generally, your basis is the amount of premiums you have paid into the policy less any dividends or withdrawals you have previously taken. Withdrawals amounts exceeding your basis is considered gains, and will be taxed as ordinary income. However, if the policy is classified as a modified endowment contract (MEC) (a situation that occurs when you put in more premiums than the threshold allows), then the gain must be withdrawn first and taxed.

Keep in mind that as you withdraw part of your cash value, the death benefit available to your survivors will be reduced.

9) **You won't have to pay taxes on loans taken against your policy.** If you take out a loan against the cash value of your insurance policy, the amount of the loan is not taxable (except in the case of an MEC). *This result is the case even if the loan is larger than the amount of the premiums you have paid in.* Such a loan is not taxed as long as the policy is in force. As you take out a loan against your policy, the death benefit and cash value of the policy will be reduced.

There it is. . . You now know the secret. The **Smart** way to withdraw your money from your Life Policy is to borrow it out. I can hear your brain thinking right now, "But, wait a minute, Laurett said I ought to 'borrow' from the death benefit and cash value of my policy. Does that mean I have to pay interest?" Here's the answer: Yes, *but*. . .Yes, there is interest assessed on the loan, however, the most recent updated policies provide that the interest rate assessed while borrowing is the same interest rate paid by the insurance company into the account, while it is borrowed out. So the policyholder is effectively borrowing the interest out at 0%. An exception to the

0% loan may be during the surrender period, which is typically the first 10 years. Companies still allow borrowing from the account, yet may credit less interest to your account during the surrender charge years. For example, you may borrow your cash out of the RAFT at 5% and the insurance company may credit to your account 3%, thus, your loan would actually cost you 2% until the surrender charge years are past.

Some companies provide 'Participating Loan' options where the policy owner can opt to borrow out at a slightly higher rate than the 'Wash Loan' but their money will remained linked to the increases in the Market. So, for example, they may borrow from the policy at 6% and the Market gains 10%. The insurance company would credit the RAFT account at 10% and charge 6% to the policy owner. In which case, the policy owner would have a net gain of 4% in his or her account. The caveat being that should the Market decline while the loan was in force, the policy owner may end up paying 6% and not getting a gain that particular year. Nobody has a crystal ball, yet we do pay attention to the historical returns and history shows that the participating loans have, on average, actually provided a higher return for the policyholders than have the wash loans (0% loans).

10) You can't deduct interest you've paid on policy loans. The interest you pay on any loans taken out against the cash value of your life insurance is not tax deductible, yet it is offset by equal earnings within the account, which are provided by the insurance company. Certain loans on business-owned policies are an exception to this rule. Abiding by tax and lending rules underscores the critical importance of designing the policy correctly, with a company that provides for Wash or Zero-spread loans.

Again, Zero is our Hero. That basically means that when you borrow from your policy, you will pay interest to the insurance company. At the same time, the insurance company will credit the same amount in your account. So to explain this in real numbers, let's say you borrow out $10,000 on an indefinite loan and the interest rate is 5% a year. You will pay $500 interest annually to borrow that $10,000; yet, the insurance company will pay you $500 interest into the cash value of your policy, as if the $10,000 is still in the account. So essentially you have paid 0% for the loan against your permanent insurance policy. We call that a 'zero spread' loan or a 'wash' loan. And it is the magic of the RAFT Strategy.

11) The surrender of your policy may result in taxable gains. If you surrender your cash value life insurance policy, any gain on the policy will be subject to federal (and possibly state) income tax. That is why we say that *surrendering* your policy is the 'Dumb' way to get your money out of your life insurance policy. The gain on the surrender of a cash value policy is the difference between the gross cash value paid out plus any loans outstanding, and your basis in the policy. Your basis is the total premiums that you paid in cash, minus any policy dividends and tax-free withdrawals that you made.

Surrendering your policy may also result in surrender charges from the insurance company, depending on how long you have had the policy in force. If you have a permanent life insurance policy that is more than 10 years old, have an SWC look at it and see if it makes sense to upgrade it into a newer, shinier model by using the IRS guideline 1035 exchange, explained in key # 12.

Now, provided the exchange is done correctly, you could even save money on the cost of insurance because men and women are projected to live longer than ever before and the real cost of life insurance has decreased. Keep in mind, however, that you have aged since you first took out the old policy, so the rates will have changed to reflect your age, but the overall cost of insurance has decreased since the new CSO* tables came out in 2001. Note, too, that insurance companies are sometimes slow to make changes, so many of the larger insurance companies took several years to adopt the new tables. Be sure that whoever produces an illustration for you is doing so using the 2001 CSO table to project mortality expenses. (The *Commissioners Standard Ordinary mortality table is an actuarial table used to compute the minimum non-forfeiture values of ordinary life insurance policies. It reflects the probability that people in various age groups will die in a given year.)

12) You may be able to exchange one policy for another without triggering tax liability. The tax code allows you to exchange one life insurance policy for another (or a life insurance policy for an annuity) without triggering current tax liability. This is known as a

Section 1035 exchange. However, you must follow the IRS's rules when making the exchange.

The tax rules surrounding life insurance are obviously complex and are subject to change. For more information, contact a qualified insurance professional, attorney, or accountant. We suggest you contact a licensed, trained and qualified SWC (perhaps the person who gave you this book) to be sure your policies are dealt with properly.

How about a bowl of alphabet soup. . .
. . .oooOOOEEEEeee. . . What's up with That?
What's up with That?

IRS Codes 101, 7702, TEFRA, DEFRA,TAMRA

Okay, I'm getting punchy. I just can't help it, when I look at all the numbers and letters governing the IRA/Insurance company integration, all I can think of is the Saturday Night Live (SNL) sketch, 'What's Up With That'. If you have no idea what I am referring to, Google it: SNL- What's Up With That? You will laugh your head off, but don't die yet, let's get your RAFT set up first.

Real quick. . . so you can't claim I didn't educate you, here are brief descriptions of the IRS codes governing tax-free distributions on life insurance policies.

- **Section 101** of the Internal Revenue Code provides that the proceeds of a life insurance policy maturing as a death claim, subject to the exceptions stated in the law, are not subject to income tax when paid. This tax benefit is one of many fundamental reasons for the growth of the life insurance industry.
- **TEFRA:** With the passage of the Tax Equity and Fiscal Responsibility Act of 1982, Congress provided a mechanism to allow Universal Life - type policies to be treated as life insurance for tax purposes, thus providing the UL policies the tax benefits of IRS Section 101 treatment. TEFRA addressed only "flexible premium" life insurance and left open the need for a statutory definition of life insurance as a whole.

- **DEFRA:** The Deficit Reduction Act of 1984 was passed. Basically, DEFRA took the TEFRA rules and modified them, providing a general set of qualifications for any contract to qualify as a life insurance policy for income tax purposes. Included were tests that effectively limited the amount of premium and required at least a minimum amount of pure risk coverage in order to qualify. Thereafter, compliance has become a matter of mathematical calculation and ongoing testing to assure policies meet the statutory definition both at issue and while it remains in force. By providing a consistent definition of life insurance, DEFRA effectively made it clear that all qualifying life insurance policies will be taxed under the favorable rules provided by the Internal Revenue Code. Basically, that means that the death proceeds of life insurance are generally received income tax free by the beneficiary. This applies to the full death benefit, including the cash value component. This means that any interest increment included in the policy cash value and death benefit is free from federal income tax when paid at death.

- **TAMRA:** The Technical and Miscellaneous Revenue Act of 1988 created a new category of life insurance policy called a Modified Endowment Contract (MEC). TAMRA defines such a contract as one which fails to meet certain premium limitation tests, first on an annual and then on a cumulative basis. The TAMRA test period runs for 7 years from the time it starts, hence its common name, the "7-Pay Test". As with TEFRA and DEFRA, compliance with TAMRA involves fairly straightforward mathematical computations performed by life insurance companies. It should be noted that death benefits of both types of policies (non-MECs and MECs) are generally paid free from income tax, including any cash value component. Policy distributions, however, are taxed differently, depending on whether or not the life insurance policy is classified as a MEC.

- **7702A:** Modified Endowment Contracts. This is any permanent policy that fails a 7-Pay Test described in IRS Code. Congress has determined that MECs must form a special

95

category of life insurance and be subject to special rules of taxation. MECs are still life insurance, but Congress considers them to be a close relative to investments because of the emphasis on tax-deferred buildup of cash values. If cash values accumulate too fast in a life insurance policy, it might be considered more of an investment vehicle than protection against premature death. Therefore, MECs enjoy some but not all of the tax advantages of regular life insurance policies. The major drawback to a MEC is the 10% federal penalty for early withdrawal prior to age 59 ½ and the fact that distributions are taxed as coming from earnings first.

In the early 1980's, the introduction of Universal Life caused some confusion. Prior to TEFRA and DEFRA, there was no specific federal law definition of life insurance. Federal taxation was governed by how the states treated the contract under their various insurance laws. If the contract met the state's requirements to be a life insurance policy, then the policy would be treated as life insurance for federal tax purposes. Universal Life uses the policy's cash value build-up to supplement future income in a client's later years which makes that cash value build-up more noticeable.

We use Equity Indexed Universal Life Insurance to fund the RAFT Strategy. Next you will see three different Illustrations for a 45 year old male, based on real numbers provided to a top insurance company. Keep in mind that women are slightly cheaper to insure than men because on average they live longer. Health issues also change death benefit amounts, but most importantly, the ratio of death benefit to cash accumulation is what determines the tax-free nature of the investment side of the RAFT. For example, a non-smoker will cost less to insure than a smoker of the same age and gender, yet the tax-free cash distributions will be very similar because the insurance company compensates by merely lowering the death benefit of the smoker. This really levels the playing field and enables a person of almost any age and health status to participate, provided the policy is approved.

Note these three variables for investing $50,000 total in the RAFT, based on 8% growth, then taking lifetime tax-free distributions starting at age 65:

(The 25 year average RoR in the RAFT has been almost 9% annually) Preferred nonsmoker funding $10,000/year for 5 years:

Age	Year	Premium	Loans	Cumul. Net Outlay	Surrender Value	Death Benefit
46	1	$10,000	$0	$10,000	$2,542	$217,817
47	2	$10,000	$0	$20,000	$12,383	$217,817
48	3	$10,000	$0	$30,000	$22,974	$217,817
49	4	$10,000	$0	$40,000	$34,381	$217,817
50	5	$10,000	$0	$50,000	$46,667	$217,817
51	6	$0	$0	$50,000	$49,656	$217,817
52	7	$0	$0	$50,000	$52,864	$217,817
53	8	$0	$0	$50,000	$56,308	$217,817
54	9	$0	$0	$50,000	$60,013	$217,817
55	10	$0	$0	$50,000	$64,002	$217,817
56	11	$0	$0	$50,000	$69,355	$217,817
57	12	$0	$0	$50,000	$75,079	$217,817
58	13	$0	$0	$50,000	$81,200	$217,817
59	14	$0	$0	$50,000	$87,749	$217,817
60	15	$0	$0	$50,000	$94,761	$217,817
61	16	$0	$0	$50,000	$102,277	$217,817
62	17	$0	$0	$50,000	$109,935	$217,817
63	18	$0	$0	$50,000	$118,194	$217,817
64	19	$0	$0	$50,000	$127,108	$217,817

65	20	$0	$0	$50,000	$136,737	$217,817
66	21	$0	$15,704	$34,296	$130,607	$201,281
67	22	$0	$15,704	$18,592	$124,453	$183,868
68	23	$0	$15,704	$2,888	$118,309	$165,532
69	24	$0	$15,704	$0	$112,217	$146,225
70	25	$0	$15,704	$0	$106,230	$137,934
71	26	$0	$15,704	$0	$100,324	$132,373
72	27	$0	$15,704	$0	$94,512	$124,462
73	28	$0	$15,704	$0	$88,836	$116,166
74	29	$0	$15,704	$0	$83,351	$107,467
75	30	$0	$15,704	$0	$78,117	$98,351

Notice the difference in the Death Benefit (DB) for the Preferred Nonsmoker of $217,817, whereas the Standard Smoker's DB is $175,351. Even though there is a big difference in the DB, the tax-free loans only differ by $1300 a year.

Standard smoker funding $10,000/year for 5 years:

Age	Year	Premium	Loans	Cumul. Net Outlay	Surrender Value	Death Benefit
46	1	$10,000	$0	$10,000	$2,719	$175,795
47	2	$10,000	$0	$20,000	$12,478	$175,795
48	3	$10,000	$0	$30,000	$22,984	$175,795
49	4	$10,000	$0	$40,000	$34,308	$175,795
50	5	$10,000	$0	$50,000	$46,518	$175,795

51	6	$0	$0	$50,000	$49,414	$175,795
52	7	$0	$0	$50,000	$52,507	$175,795
53	8	$0	$0	$50,000	$55,806	$175,795
54	9	$0	$0	$50,000	$59,315	$175,795
55	10	$0	$0	$50,000	$63,050	$175,795
56	11	$0	$0	$50,000	$67,972	$175,795
57	12	$0	$0	$50,000	$73,200	$175,795
58	13	$0	$0	$50,000	$78,756	$175,795
59	14	$0	$0	$50,000	$84,690	$175,795
60	15	$0	$0	$50,000	$91,037	$175,795
61	16	$0	$0	$50,000	$97,852	$175,795
62	17	$0	$0	$50,000	$104,783	$175,795
63	18	$0	$0	$50,000	$112,280	$175,795
64	19	$0	$0	$50,000	$120,398	$175,795
65	20	$0	$0	$50,000	$129,203	$175,795
66	21	$0	$14,345	$35,655	$123,666	$160,690
67	22	$0	$14,345	$21,310	$118,186	$146,534
68	23	$0	$14,345	$6,965	$112,826	$141,732
69	24	$0	$14,345	$0	$107,448	$136,831
70	25	$0	$14,345	$0	$102,069	$131,835
71	26	$0	$14,345	$0	$96,715	$126,750
72	27	$0	$14,345	$0	$91,440	$119,462
73	28	$0	$14,345	$0	$86,296	$111,826
74	29	$0	$14,345	$0	$81,345	$103,842

Notice how compressing the $50,000 total contribution into 5 years rather than spreading it out over 10 years, as in our next example, jump starts the compounding effect and therefore increases the projected distributions by almost 50%. Also, notice below that the distributions don't stop. I just showed the first ten years to save space in the book. Stretching out the above example to age 90 would show the $50,000 investment blossoming into $358,625 of tax-free distributions by age 90, which is roughly equal to $500K tax-deferred.

Standard nonsmoker funding $5,000/year for 10 years:

Age	Year	Premium	Loans	Cumul. Net Outlay	Surrender Value	Death Benefit
46	1	$5,000	$0	$5,000	$0	$215,659
47	2	$5,000	$0	$10,000	$1,643	$215,659
48	3	$5,000	$0	$15,000	$6,159	$215,659
49	4	$5,000	$0	$20,000	$10,992	$215,659
50	5	$5,000	$0	$25,000	$16,164	$215,659
51	6	$5,000	$0	$30,000	$21,721	$215,659
52	7	$5,000	$0	$35,000	$27,691	$215,659
53	8	$5,000	$0	$40,000	$34,105	$215,659
54	9	$5,000	$0	$45,000	$41,002	$215,659
55	10	$5,000	$0	$50,000	$48,420	$215,659
56	11	$0	$0	$50,000	$52,387	$215,659
57	12	$0	$0	$50,000	$56,596	$215,659
58	13	$0	$0	$50,000	$61,063	$215,659
59	14	$0	$0	$50,000	$65,802	$215,659

60	15	$0	$0	$50,000	$70,833	$215,659
61	16	$0	$0	$50,000	$76,192	$215,659
62	17	$0	$0	$50,000	$81,504	$215,659
63	18	$0	$0	$50,000	$87,207	$215,659
65	19	$0	$0	$50,000	$93,338	$215,659
65	20	$0	$0	$50,000	$99,934	$215,659
66	21	$0	$10,977	$39,023	$95,475	$204,100
67	22	$0	$10,977	$28,046	$90,954	$191,929
68	23	$0	$10,977	$17,069	$86,390	$179,112
69	24	$0	$10,977	$6,092	$81,804	$165,617
70	25	$0	$10,977	$0	$77,229	$151,406
71	26	$0	$10,977	$0	$72,699	$136,441
72	27	$0	$10,977	$0	$68,236	$120,684
73	28	$0	$10,977	$0	$63,900	$104,092
74	29	$0	$10,977	$0	$59,762	$86,620
75	30	$0	$10,977	$0	$55,917	$70,152
76	31	$0	$10,977	$0	$52,486	$63,451
77	32	$0	$10,977	$0	$49,306	$61,132
78	33	$0	$10,977	$0	$46,373	$59,127
79	34	$0	$10,977	$0	$43,725	$57,477
80	35	$0	$10,977	$0	$41,401	$56,228
81	36	$0	$10,977	$0	$39,446	$55,428
82	37	$0	$10,977	$0	$37,908	$55,134

83	38	$0	$10,977	$0	$36,838	$55,402
84	39	$0	$10,977	$0	$36,288	$56,288
85	40	$0	$10,977	$0	$36,308	$57,850
86	41	$0	$10,977	$0	$36,933	$60,130
87	42	$0	$10,977	$0	$38,193	$63,163
88	43	$0	$10,977	$0	$40,118	$66,985
89	44	$0	$10,977	$0	$42,731	$71,623
90	45	$0	$10,977	$0	$46,040	$77,094

As you can see, our 45 Year old nonsmoker was able to turn a $50,000 investment into tax-free distributions equaling $274,425. Is this a guarantee? Not at all; yet, it does illustrate, based on real numbers how the RAFT can be used to benefit the policyholder and the beneficiaries. As long as the policy stays in force, the owner can borrow money out faster, sooner, later, or repay the loan to accumulate more growth. You can see how the death benefit started at $215,659 and gradually decreased as tax-free distributions come out of the account. In addition to tax-free safety, liquidity, and a great rate of return, there is beauty in the flexibility of the RAFT contract.

Also, you may have caught on that in the last few years the death benefit is edging up again. This is because the interest created in the RAFT is surpassing the distributions coming out. I only showed up to age 90, yet according to the illustration, the distributions last into perpetuity. So don't worry about outliving your money. Just keep taking the tax-free distributions and enjoy your life! Remember, the illustration is just an idea of how the money can come out. It is not rigid and there are countless ways to extract the money, once the cash has accumulated in the RAFT.

I only shared with you a few examples of an illustration an SWC can provide. Keep in mind that the RAFT can be funded a number of ways using money from a wide variety of sources, totally depending on the circumstances and needs of the individual applying for the coverage. Just remember that the contributions are done with after-tax money.

Maybe you don't have a lump sum to move into the RAFT. That's Okay. It can be funded on a monthly basis. Maybe you have a savings or money market account you can use to fund the RAFT. Maybe you have a CD that is about to mature and you do not want to place that money back on the *SHOCK* market. Now is your chance to take a portion of your nest egg and position it for tax free growth, while experiencing the Lock-in and Reset that protects your asset. You may be thinking you will have to build up your nest egg little by little, on a monthly basis. That works too. The key is to have an expert run the numbers so you can develop a plan that is best for you.

Maybe you have an old life insurance policy that is not getting a great return for you. Remember that as long a policy holder qualifies for a new insurance policy, the cash value from one permanent life insurance policy can be transferred, directly into another, without a tax consequence? This is employing the 1035 exchange and it is a good way to upgrade existing coverage so you can begin driving around your newer, shinier, more productive RAFT policy.

Suffice it to say, a properly designed and funded EIUL is one of the most attractive financial products someone can consider. What I'm presenting here is only an overview. As with any discussion of products and taxes, there are always exceptions to the general rules. Remember, this is YOUR Future. YOU are in charge. Don't let this idea slip through your fingers. It is likely good for you or someone close to you. I hear this all the time, "Laurett, I wish I would have done this years ago. If only I had known about it then." Well, now is your opportunity to engage. Do it now before life gets in the way, again.

It is simple to contact us and it takes only a few minutes to fill out a trial application. Hey, I don't know if the insurance company is going to accept you. I don't know your health issues. Sometimes I am surprised that someone is turned down, based on something I have no idea about and sometimes something they had no clue of. I always say, applying for the RAFT is much like applying for a job. You really don't know if they will offer you the position, until you try, and even then you have to like the job before you'll accept. Correct?

Basically our SWCs just take down some very basic information from you. They schedule a paramedic (may be a nurse) to come to your home and do a quick physical exam. The examiner sends the blood and urine samples to the lab and the lab reports the results to the insurance company. Based on the results of the tests, the interview with the proposed insured, and the paper application the insurance agent provides; the insurance company underwriters make a decision whether or not to insure that individual. They then contact the agent (SWC) and give them their decision.

Next, the SWC contacts YOU, the proposed insured, and informs you if the policy you designed together was accepted or denied by the insurance company. Maybe it was accepted, but changed because of issues they found during the application process. You truly won't know until you try. Put us to work and the RAFT will work for you. It is simple to do, yet simple to delay. . . Just Do IT.

Chapter 7

Second Jewel of the Triple Crown Solution: Triple P (Personal Pension Plan) With Principal Protection

I cannot tell you how many times listeners have called our office and asked, "Why have I not heard about the RAFT strategy before?" or they'll comment, "I wish I would have known of these concepts 20 & 30 years ago." All I can say is that the time is NOW. You still have time to fix your future, provided you take action or educate those in your life who can.

Let me remind you that the RAFT Strategy did not existed in its present form until the late 1990s when Indexed Universal Life was introduced. Most new concepts that reach widespread acceptance go through a period of pioneering until about 10% of the population is educated on the idea. Then, as the concept is further embraced, momentum pushes the idea to the next level of consciousness which creates a critical mass, or flash point, and eventually the idea achieves universal acknowledgement.

As the first Baby Boomers turned 66 years old in 2012, the whole generation stepped into a new phase of life. This massive people bubble born between 1946 and 1964 has driven every market for the past 50+ years. Now they are retiring to the tune of 10,000+ per day. The sad news is that only a fraction of them are truly prepared. Had the RAFT Strategy existed in its present form and had they been astute enough to engage, we may be seeing a different picture today. Yet, we cannot go back and change things. The best we can do is to move forward armed with knowledge and resolve to do what it takes to create the future we want.

Now, before I introduce to you the second Jewel of the Triple Crown solution, I want to acknowledge that the RAFT Strategy is not a perfect fit for everyone because not all those who want to engage in it can qualify for the EIUL. In fact, as I mentioned in Chapter 6, I look at the process of applying for an insurance policy kind of like applying for a job. You never know if you will be offered the policy until after the underwriters have gone through your medical history, driver's record, and health status. Even when you are offered the policy from the insurance company, you still have the option to take it or not. There is no risk in applying for coverage so you can start the RAFT. It doesn't cost a penny to apply. Just be sure that the adviser, who helps you set up you RAFT, does so using the Guideline Premium for Minimum Face (Death Benefit) and Maximum Cash Accumulation. That very simply means that the policy is written for the least amount of insurance combined with the most amount of cash the policy owner wants to place in the policy. So first we decide how much money we want to set aside in the RAFT, and according to IRS guidelines, the face amount will be determined in ratio to the cash placed inside the policy. It is done with special software supplied by insurance companies to licensed SWCs and according to individual state regulations.

Some who love the idea of the RAFT, because of their age, may not have a long enough time horizon to fund the policy, allow it to grow and borrow enough tax-free distributions for the RAFT to work effectively. For this reason, I typically recommend starting the RAFT prior to age 65 unless someone has a permanent life insurance policy (Whole or Variable Life) with cash value that they can transfer into the new EIUL using the IRS Provision 1035 exchange we touched on previously. The 1035 exchange would jumpstart the new EIUL, thus creating an instant RAFT.

So where does that leave those of you who are over 65 or who have health issues, such that you don't qualify for the RAFT? Have you missed the boat (or in this case, the life-RAFT) entirely? Not at all; we have a solution for you in the form of Fixed Indexed Annuities (FIAs.) They come in all shapes and sizes with a number of bells and whistles. On the radio show we refer to the FIA category as the Triple P (PPP-*Personal Pension Plan*) Program. I consider the PPP to be similar to a pension plan funded through your company or employer, but the PPP is funded by the individual and may use money transferred from a traditional qualified retirement plan, or set up as a non-qualified plan with after-taxed money. Like the RAFT, it's another way to take control of your financial future. The PPP works especially well for those between 40 and 80 years old and can be opened as a qualified or a non-qualified annuity.

As you may have guessed, as SWCs, we first explore the merits of the RAFT as part of our client's investment portfolio. Next, we look at what *qualified* investments he or she already has. Then we look at non-qualified money that may be best placed in PPP because the investor is not well suited for the RAFT. Our goal is to help our clients protect and perpetuate their assets overall. Remembering that the RAFT is funded with non-qualified (after-tax) money, that leaves the tax-deferred accounts like IRAs, TSPs, 403(b)s, 401(k)s and 457 plans and others in a totally different investment category. (Going forward, I will refer to these qualified plans as IRAs.)

Idiomatically speaking, the RAFT is an Apple and the PPP is an Orange. They can both be in the same fruit salad, but genetically they don't mix. When was the last time you went to the farmers market and saw an Aporange or an Orple? The answer is: Never. Apples don't breed with oranges. The truth is that apples and oranges have more similarities than they do differences; like both are fruit and both grow on trees. Yet, somehow they are different enough that we don't put them in the same category.

Clients frequently surmise that they can take the money from their IRA or 401(k) to fund the RAFT. It *can* be done, provided we jump through the proper hoops. The RAFT can be funded without penalty after age 59 ½, provided the income tax on the money taken from the IRA to fund the RAFT is paid. We call that way of funding the RAFT from a qualified account a 'Strategic Roll-Out'. It can be a good idea for those who have reached 59 ½ years old and want to aggressively fund the RAFT. Note that typically, withdrawals from an IRA or other tax-qualified plan, prior to age 59 ½, will incur a 10% additional tax or what most of us refer to as an 'early withdrawal penalty'. However, an individual can take penalty free withdrawals from their IRA prior to age 59 ½ under certain circumstances, including that contained in section 72(t) of IRS code.

IRS code 72(t) allows for penalty free withdrawals prior to age 59 ½ from qualified retirement approaches by following exact guidelines using Substantially Equal Periodic Payments (SEPP). According to the rule, penalty- free withdrawals are allowed provided the money is accessed in equal payments, over at least a five year period of time. Income tax is still due on the withdrawals from the qualified plan. Once the tax is paid, the funds can be placed into the RAFT Strategy, where the account will grow tax-free, as long as it is designed, funded, and accessed, according to proper IRS guidelines.

There are a few methods for determining the annual withdrawal from an IRA prior to age 59 ½ utilizing 72(t). Part of this IRS guideline limits the percentage one can take from their IRA based on their life expectancy. The chart below illustrates that even though 72(t) allows for penalty-free early withdrawal, the annual distribution prior to age 59 ½ is limited and can change based on your age, rate of interest, age of beneficiary and chosen calculation method. An SWC can calculate this number for you. Also, in the resource section of this book, we have also included references to online calculators that can assist you.

Account balance	$100,000
Your age	50
Beneficiary age	45
Applicable life expectancy	34.2 single life expectancy
Maximum distribution	$6,161
Method used	Fixed amortization method
Interest rate used	5%

Before engaging 72(t), be sure you understand you options and how each may affect your annual penalty-free distribution.

Now let's get back to the second Jewel of the Triple Crown Solution, the PPP Program. As I mentioned earlier, the PPP refers to a category of annuities called Fixed Indexed Annuities (FIAs). Why do I endorse FIAs? Well, it goes back to the same Lock-in and Reset principal I shared with you in Chapter 5. When I know I can experience gains in my investments that are linked to the equity markets without experiencing losses when the Markets are down, I can sleep at night because my retirement approach is going nowhere but UP!

All Annuities are not Created Equal

At times we get calls from listeners who state, "If this is an Annuity, I'm not interested." Invariably, when I mention a few features of the annuities we endorse, the caller exclaims something like this, "Now that is nothing like I have experienced or learned about annuities so far in my life." That may be the case because annuities have evolved dramatically over the past decade. If you are thinking about the old school annuity that your father owned; the one that could experience losses and didn't provide a death benefit, I'm not surprised that you would rather pass on the idea.

The word 'Annuity' is a noun and can be defined in modern terms three different ways:

- A fixed sum of money paid to someone (an annuitant) each year, typically for the rest of their life.
- A form of insurance or investment entitling the investor to a series of annual income payments.
- Longevity Insurance (My favorite because annuities protect the annuitant by ensuring they won't run out of money during their lifetime.)

I'm just going to showcase the basic types of annuities - Fixed, Variable and Indexed. You will get educated on this annuity evolution that has taken place. My guess is that you will see that there may be a place in your retirement portfolio for one brand of annuity or another.

It all starts with Fixed Annuities (FAs) which have existed through insurance companies for over two centuries. They were a small part of the insurance business until the Roaring 20s when employers and insurance companies teamed up to provide a path to lifetime income for employees. FAs gained momentum during the Great Depression because people saw the benefit of having a guaranteed income for life. A very conservative approach to retirement planning, FAs provide a fixed rate of return similar to that of a Certificate of Deposit (CD) from a bank. The main difference being that an annuity typically guarantees a much higher interest rate than a CD and the interest in an annuity compounds from year to year, growing tax-deferred; whereas, interest in a CD is subject to annual capital gains tax.

There are a variety of options for accruing interest in CDs and annuities. Some CDs pay monthly, others pay quarterly or annually. The owner of the CD may have an option to reinvest the interest into the CD or take it out. CDs also have penalties for early withdrawal based on the term of the CD. Similarly, the owner of an annuity typically has the option to take up to 10% of the basis (initial deposit) out every year, without penalty. An annuity is a savings/investment account and contract with an insurance company. As with any insurance policy or contract, each annuity has a 'term' which is called a 'surrender period'.

A surrender period may be as little as 7 years and as much as 17 years, depending on the annuity. Most often we see annuities with a 10 year surrender period. For example, any year the owner withdraws more than 10%, the amount taken beyond 10% may be subject to a penalty, which decreases every year. Below is an example of a simple 10 year decreasing surrender charge for a life insurance policy or annuity contract:

Year	1	2	3	4	5	6	7	8	9	10	11
Charge	10%	10%	9%	8%	7%	6%	5%	4%	3%	2%	0%

In real numbers, let's say you have placed $100,000 in a fixed annuity with an interest rate of 3% and a 10 year surrender charge. Next, let's say you take out 20% after the first year anniversary, which is the same date that it was issued, one year later. Well, 10% (half of the amount you withdrew) will be sent to you with no penalty. The other half of the amount you withdrew will have a 10% penalty (surrender charge) assessed, so the insurance company will still send you $20,000, but there would be a $1,000 surrender charge subtracted from the accumulation value (cash value) of the annuity. You would have accrued 3% interest in the account ($3,000). Add the $3,000 to the remaining $79,000, and the cash value on the annuity would be $82,000. $100,000 - $20,000 - $1,000 + $3,000 = $82,000.

Using the same surrender charge table, and the same $100,000, but waiting 6 years before taking the same withdrawal, the surrender charge penalty would be 5% on 10% of the basis. Your request for $20,000 from your account would only incur a $500 surrender charge within the fixed annuity contract. Your cash value at that point would be based on your principal deposit of $100,000 plus the 3% compounded growth, minus the $20,000 withdrawal, and minus $500 surrender charge. The math looks like this: $100,000 compounded for 6 years at 3% = $119,405.23 - $20,000 - $500 = $98,905.23 total cash value in your fixed annuity. That's pretty simple, right? The other types of annuities get a bit more complicated, yet they will have similar surrender charges and still grow tax-deferred.

In summary, a fixed annuity has 5 main benefits.

1) Guaranteed Rate of Return
2) Protection against Loss (Safety)
3) Tax-Deferred Growth
4) Flexible withdrawal options
5) Optional Guaranteed Income for life

I have said many times that opening a Fixed Annuity with a life insurance company is a lot like opening a CD or money market account with a bank, although it comes with much higher rate of return and the option for *guaranteed income for life*. That's right; I said **guaranteed** income for life, which is the true purpose of annuities to begin with. Although not mandatory, all annuities provide an option for the owner to turn on an income stream that will last as long as he or she lives. Most annuities also provide an option for a 'joint' payout, meaning that when the annuitant (typically the owner of the contract) passes on, his or her spouse can continue receiving payments for the rest of her or his life as well.

The benefit of joint income is that both partners have the security of knowing they will receive a certain amount of income as long as they live. A drawback to receiving joint income could be that the payment would be less because the insurance company is providing 'Longevity Insurance' for two individuals, instead of one. Also, the payment is based on the age of the younger spouse. Since the younger spouse is expected to receive payments for a longer period of time than the older partner, the insurance company reduces the annual payout based on the younger spouse's age.

Some of the newer annuities provide for increasing income, which means that the annual payment can actually increase from year to year as interest credits are locked into the account, according to the contract. These interest credits are typically linked to the growth of mutual funds or equity indexes, which brings us to the second type of annuity, the Variable.

My emotions are all over the place when I think of Variable Annuities (VA), maybe because the returns on a VA are all over the place. Remember that a fixed annuity is a safe, conservative investment and acts much like a CD, well, a VA resembles a mutual fund with all the intrinsic risk and volatility that goes alongside investing in the *SHOCK* market. When our money is invested in mutual funds, we get that adrenaline rush when the Market is up. But when we pick up the morning paper and read that the *SHOCK* market tanked, baby, it feels like morning sickness all over again.

VAs first became available in the 1950s and truly saw their heyday in the 1990s when the equity markets rallied year after year. VAs are typically invested in stocks, bonds and mutual funds, so they can experience aggressive growth. Many investors like the idea of combining equity market returns with the tax-deferred growth annuities provide. For a younger investor, VAs may have their place because the investor who wants to potentially get a high RoR and has several years before retirement, in case the investment goes south. Here's where the 'Rule of 100' kicks in. The Rule of 100 as I explained in Chapter 2, is a basic mathematical formula widely used by financial professionals for determining how much of one's nest egg should be placed in a risk position. Ask yourself how much of your nest egg you feel you can expose to risk for the opportunity of possibly higher returns.

I'm slightly biased here because for years, we have recommended only investments that provide principal guarantees, and the VA is not one of those. I do see the attraction of VAs because they provide a solid death benefit and have a potential for high gains, but there are two major challenges: Risk and Fees. VAs have all the fees associated with traditional money management on top of potential surrender charges. (Surrender charge periods on VAs are usually shorter than on other annuities; typically 5-7 years.) Also, I cannot conceive why someone would elect to house their money in a risk environment, when they could have the best of both worlds; i.e., market-like returns along with principal guarantees. This all brings us up to date with the newest, shiniest model of annuity that exists today, the Equity Indexed Annuity (EIA) aka Fixed Indexed Annuity (FIA). (Going forward, I will use EIA in discussing this newest kid on the block, so as not to be confused with aforementioned Fixed Annuity (FA) category)

The EIA comes in many shapes and sizes. *And these ain't your Grandma's annuities!* They have been designed by truly prodigious insurance actuaries. There are so many bells, whistles, and variations within these new annuities because every insurance company wants to remain competitive with the next company. The most important features of the EIA are very similar to those in the RAFT and are listed here:

1) Principal Guarantees
2) Lock-in of gains every year and reset of the index
3) Returns are linked to equity market growth

4) Annual rebalancing options within the account
5) No fees in most basic products
6) Free withdrawals
7) Decreasing surrender charges
8) Death benefit
9) Tax-Deferred growth
10) Lifetime income options

When I think back to 2007 when we were opening EIAs for clients all over the country, I remember that some of our wide-eyed believers took the plunge on 'faith' and opened an EIA for the first time. When we told them they could move their money from an old 401(k) into an IRA with this certain EIA and get a 20% upfront bonus they were intrigued. When we shared that the annual returns in the account would be linked to the gains in the equity markets, they were excited. When we showed them that the insurance company guaranteed they would not lose a penny due to losses in the *SHOCK* market, they were elated. And finally, when we announced that they could get all that value without paying any fees, they were downright ecstatic.

Could it really be true? Well, they found out the next year (2008) when the Market plunged, that is *was* true. I cannot tell you how many of our clients expressed gratitude during their annual review that they had made the decision to start their PPP Program with the EIA we recommended. When we went over their statements; that 'faith' turned into belief when our clients saw that their IRA did not suffer losses, while their neighbor's IRA took a 35% hit. On top of that, in 2009, when the *SHOCK* market bounced back, our clients received 7-24% increases, depending on how their annuity was linked to the indices and allocated within the account.

Now, I mentioned a 'bonus'. Some insurance companies provide annuities that include a bonus or a match; akin to how an employer may match contributions within a 401(k) plan. For example, with a 20% bonus, when a $100,000 contribution is made into the account, the insurance company will deposit $20,000 on top of the $100,000 making the principal $120,000 available for future distributions.

Typically the bonus vests over a period of time (perhaps 10 years), so it is available for distribution to the EIA owner after 10 years. The bonus, principal and interest are accessible, in accordance with the parameters of the EIA. I have seen bonuses as little as 2% and as much as 25%, with varying vesting periods.

You might be thinking, "As Laurett describes it, there seems to be no drawback to the EIA. Why wouldn't everyone move their 401(k), IRA or even money in a savings account or the stock market over to the PPP?" The answer is simple: *They don't know about it yet*. Also, I admit, there are a few caveats. Remember surrender charges? They do exist in all annuities, so the money is only partially liquid. Also, there are caps (limits) on the upside potential. These caps vary from product to product, but can dissuade a more aggressive investor from wanting to engage. For example, let's say there is a 5% annual cap in the EIA and it is linked to the S&P 500. Now let's say that the S&P 500 grew 8% in one year, as measured on the anniversary date of the contract. The interest credits received in the account would be 5%. Because of the Lock-in and Reset feature in an EIA, the interest credit becomes part of the new principal amount. So does the 'cap' really limit the overall growth? It is a matter of opinion. After you see the upcoming charts, you decide.

The graph below shows the volatility of the S&P 500 for a 15 year period of time, from January 1st 1998, to January 1st 2013. With a starting principal amount of $10,000, the dotted line shows the movement of the S&P 500. Assuming the $10,000 deposit remained in the S&P 500, we see the overall growth of about 50%. Now, notice the solid line. Assuming a 5% annual cap, it shows almost 60% growth locked into an EIA over the same period of time. The growth in the PPP resembles a stair step or an uphill climb because of the principal guarantees.

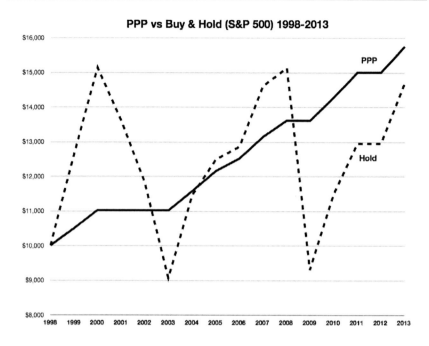

PPP vs Buy & Hold (S&P 500) 1998-2013

I have seen caps on annuities change over the years. Insurance companies, like banks, determine interest rates and caps based on movement in the US Treasury, CPI, and the general economy. When interest rates are higher, caps are usually higher as well. When they drop, so do caps. I chose to show a 5% cap because it is the average annual cap rate I have seen since EIAs came into existence in 1998. With that said, I have also seen much higher returns utilizing other crediting methods, like monthly sum or monthly averaging. I am not going to go into all the detail of the various crediting methods right here because it would fill up another book. In addition, crediting methods are constantly changing as insurance actuaries continually come up with more innovative ideas. So now would be a good time to make a note to yourself to ask your SWC about your options.

What if you had purchased the $100,000 annuity with the 5% annual cap, right at the beginning of the new millennium, after the large gains that happened in the 90s? The choice is very clear. Over the 13 year period, from 2000 until 2013, your principal still would have been protected during the 5 declining years. And your account still would have experienced the upside of the growth during the increasing years, as shown. When factoring in the rate of inflation, the S&P 500 is still not close to passing it's year 2000 high point.

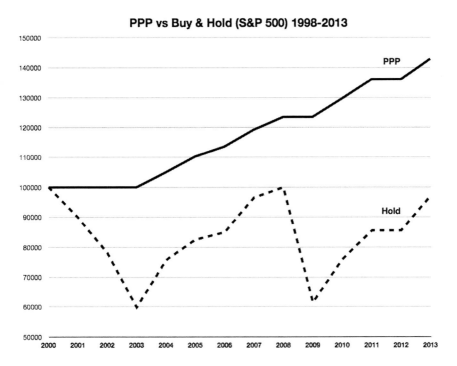

As we look at the above examples of market performance vs. the Lock-in and Reset principle, we see that there were several years that the S&P 500 outperformed the PPP, yet the PPP steadily gained. The peace of mind that comes with not having to time the Market (trying to figure out when to sell because the Market is up and when to buy because the Market is down) is extremely liberating. This reminds me of the classic Aesop's Fable 'Tortoise and Hare', where the Market is the Hare and the PPP is the Tortoise. Well, we know who ultimately wins that race!

In general, EIAs offer several choices for linking the growth of the indices to the account. Crediting methods may include Annual Point to Point, Monthly Point to Point, and Monthly Averaging with an Annual spread, to name a few. The indices vary as well. Growth could be linked to the S&P 500, the NASDAQ 100, FTSE, Barclays

Aggregate Bond, Dow Jones Industrial average, or a blend of different indices, for example. There are many options when exploring and choosing an EIA; too varied to explain fully in this book. For this reason, we suggest getting more detailed information based on your needs from a qualified SWC. If you do not yet have an SWC with whom you are personally working, be sure to contact us through our website: www.RAFTStrategy.com. We can connect you with an SWC licensed in your State.

In the next chapter we are going to show you some illustrations based on a variety of PPP Programs. But before we do, I just want to mention the golden nugget of the PPP: Longevity Insurance. No, I am not speaking of Long Term Care (LTC) Insurance; I am speaking of Income Riders. An income rider on an annuity gives the annuitant a guaranteed interest level which compounds into separate, likely much higher 'income value' which is the basis for income for life.

The distributions from an income rider are similar to annuitization, but the potential for higher income is much greater, because the income account grows to higher value before distributions begin. As in annuitizing, once the annuitant turns on the income (starts getting distributions), the income will continue every year (or month, however it is set up). Even if the cash value of the account is completely depleted, the insurance company will continue paying the annuitant for the rest of their life, and provided 'joint' income was selected, the insurance company will continue to pay the surviving spouse through life's end, as well.

Income distributions are based on the initial age of the annuitant and how long the compounded interest 'rolls-up'. The rate of distribution increases with the age of the annuitant. When taking joint income, the age of the younger spouse determines the withdrawal rate. In the next chapter, we will show some complete illustrations, however, here is a simple example of how an income rider might work:

Owner/Annuitant age: 60 (Spouse age: 55)
Initial Deposit: $100,000
Income Rider Rate: 6% annual compound interest
10 year deferred growth = $179,084.77 income base.

Single income withdrawal at the rate of 6% annually=$10,746.
Lifetime Joint income withdrawal at 5%=$8,954.

20 year deferred growth = $ 320,714.55 income base.
Single income withdrawal at the rate of 7% annually=$22,450.
Lifetime Joint income withdrawal at 6%=$19,243.

For the privilege of receiving the guaranteed high interest rate, there is typically a fee assessed against the death benefit or accumulation value of the account of .05% to 1.2%, depending on the product. In some products, fees can also be assessed for the option of receiving an enhanced Death Benefit, which could be used for legacy planning. As you can see; there are many options and it can be very confusing, yet with the assistance of the qualified SWC, you can find the answer that is best for you and your family.

I believe insurance companies have done a good job of answering the needs of an aging population, especially over the past decade. Annuities have been key partners in preserving, protecting and perpetuating millions of hard earned nest eggs. I look at the evolution of annuities like the old saying: Good, Better, Best. . . Never let it rest; until your good gets better and your better becomes best.

Chapter 8

Planning Your Future
With the 'PPP' Program

B ecause I am a numbers girl, this is a fun chapter for me. I am constantly pouring over illustrations of how the RAFT Strategy or the PPP Programs will work for my potential clients. I also teach SWCs everyday how important it is to know exactly how a PPP Program is projected to distribute money based on the initial deposit, average RoR, and when the client expects to use the money. This I know: No two cases are exactly alike. In fact, I look at illustrations as a road map to your financial retirement vacation spot and your SWC as your tour guide. The annual review your SWC provides, free of charge, is like a global positioning system (GPS) because it keeps you informed and on track to arrive at your chosen financial destination.

I had a friend named Jeff who is no longer with us. When asked how he was, Jeff would often reply, "Every day's a Holiday." I received a phone call from his wife just a few months ago and she told me that his Earthly 'Holiday' had been cut short at the young age of 50. God bless him. Nobody knows how long we will be around to enjoy our friends and family. And for some of us, every day *is* a Holiday. I've always looked at life as a journey to be enjoyed along the way, not a waiting game only to be happy when we have everything we desire. I prefer "Are we having fun?" to, "Are we there yet?" Provided we believe that the journey is just as important as the final destination, we want to have a plan that gives us that POM POM we so richly deserve. Through the following mathematical illustrations I am going to attempt to unveil some of the mystery behind what types of PPP may work best for certain age groups. I will also refer to income riders as LIP (Longevity Insurance Protection).

First, let's look at the pre-retirees: those of us in our fifties who wonder if Social Security will still be around when it is our turn at the trough. What are we looking for? Well, for me, I want to know that my qualified accounts are on track to grow and earn, not crash and burn. I don't want to see my hard earned cash flushed down the proverbial vortex of Market decline, inflation, and higher tax rates. I want the rising tide of principal protection, locked-in gains, tax-deferred growth and LIP to determine my financial destination.

So, when I looked for a place to house my IRA (which I had started prior to learning about the RAFT), I chose a PPP that would give me the option of taking a lump sum at age 59 ½, or continue to grow as I took lifetime income. The following illustration is based on placing $100,000 into the parameters of my PPP Program, linked to a twenty year look-back of the Market, and utilizing the LIP provision. In other words, had my PPP existed 20 years ago, my investment would have grown and the lifetime income distributions would have increased, as shown below:

Year Ending	Age	Net Premium	Credited Interest	Accumulation Value	Surrender Value	Guaranteed Min. Value	Withdraw Rate	Lifetime Income
11/12/1983	50	$100K	11.44%	$110,272	$99,245	$87,624	3.00%	$0
11/12/1984	51	$0	0.00%	$109,114	$98,203	$87,640	3.30%	$0
11/12/1985	52	$0	3.99%	$112,274	$102,450	$87,669	3.60%	$0
11/12/1986	53	$0	11.23%	$123,574	$114,306	$87,665	3.90%	$0
11/12/1987	54	$0	0.00%	$122,276	$114,634	$87,542	4.20%	$0
11/12/1988	55	$0	0.00%	$120,992	$114,943	$87,430	4.50%	$0
11/12/1989	56	$0	17.33%	$140,471	$135,203	$87,331	4.80%	$0

121

11/12/1990	57	$0	0.00%	$138,996	$135,521	$87,024	5.10%	$0
11/12/1991	58	$0	5.23%	$144,727	$142,918	$86,729	5.40%	$0
11/12/1992	59	$0	0.00%	$143,208	$143,208	$86,369	5.70%	$0
11/12/1993	60	$0	9.40%	$155,030	$155,030	$85,721	6.00%	$0
11/12/1994	61	$0	0.00%	$153,402	$153,402	$84,942	6.30%	$0
11/12/1995	62	$0	17.81%	$178,829	$178,829	$84,172	6.60%	$0
11/12/1996	63	$0	4.21%	$184,404	$184,404	$83,125	6.90%	$0
11/12/1997	64	$0	0.00%	$169,191	$169,191	$68,600	7.20%	$13,277
11/12/1998	65	$0	0.00%	$154,137	$154,137	$54,090		$13,277
11/12/1999	66	$0	0.00%	$139,242	$139,242	$39,594		$13,277
11/12/2000	67	$0	0.00%	$124,503	$124,503	$25,110		$13,277
11/12/2001	68	$0	0.00%	$109,918	$109,918	$10,637		$13,277
11/12/2002	69	$0	0.00%	$95,487	$95,487	$0		$13,277
11/12/2003	70	$0	0.00%	$81,207	$81,207	$0		$13,277
11/12/2004	71	$0	0.00%	$67,077	$67,077	$0		$13,277
11/12/2005	72	$0	0.00%	$53,096	$53,096	$0		$13,277
11/12/2006	73	$0	6.73%	$41,903	$41,903	$0		$13,277
11/12/2007	74	$0	0.00%	$27,292	$27,292	$0		$14,170
11/12/2008	75	$0	0.00%	$12,836	$12,836	$0		$14,170
11/12/2009	76	$0	0.00%	$0	$0	$0		$14,170
11/12/2010	77	$0	0.00%	$0	$0	$0		$14,170
11/12/2011	78	$0	0.00%	$0	$0	$0		$14,170
11/12/2012	79	$0	0.00%	$0	$0	$0		$14,170

I don't expect you to understand all of the numbers above. Just note five important aspects to this particular PPP using the LIP:

1. The withdrawal rate increases every year, so the longer I wait to take lifetime withdrawals, the higher the distribution will be.
2. The Accumulation Value and the Surrender Value are the same after the 10th year because the surrender charge has declined every year for 10 years until it is Zero %.
3. The Lifetime Income increases when interest credits are locked into the account and never decreases. I look at the annual distributions like this: My *last* withdrawal is my *worst* withdrawal. Distributions can never go down, even if the Market declines year after year.
4. My initial deposit was $100,000. I started taking distributions in the 15th year at the rate of $13,277 and in year 24, the annual distribution increased to $14,170. The insurance company ends up giving ALL my own money back to me within 8 years and in my opinion, anything above $100,000 I receive from them, is gravy.
5. Let's say I live to be 95 years old and the index option I have chosen bumps up in the 10th year and then it doesn't return any interest for the next 20 years. That's right. I get zero, zilch, zippo interest credits for 20 years. Still, the insurance company has contracted to pay me LIP of $14,170 every year, until I die.

   Guess what the total 30 year payout would be? Brrrrrr. . . Drum Roll. . . . The answer is: $416,170. My investment of $100,000 would yield over $400,000 in distributions, courtesy of my trusted insurance company. Frankly, based on my current health status, and my desire to get things done, I plan on living way past 95 so the insurance company can plan on paying me way more than $416,170. To show my appreciation for their terrific plan, I may even send a letter like this:

August 7, 2056

Dear Insurance Company,

Today I am 95 years old and I just wanted to send a note to thank you for quadrupling my retirement nest egg! My money is lasting as long as I am. I have never been a burden to my children and I sleep well every night knowing that however long I live, you will be there for me. I haven't had to worry, so life has been fabulous.

I am very grateful that I listened to my SWC and decided to set up my LIP (Longevity Insurance Protection) way back in my 50s. I've been able to enjoy myself and travel with my family. I spend the money that is outside of my PPP with ease because I know my day to day expenses are taken care of through my PPP program and my RAFT Strategy. Thanks again! Please keep doing what you are doing.

Sincerely,
Freedom Financial Angel
Laurett Ellsworth Arenz

Remember that the PPP exists in hundreds of forms, and can be set up with many different insurance companies. The illustrations I share are real and accurate, and yet, every person's situation is different, so the numbers change with each illustration. Now let's look at a scenario for a 60 year old.

I often hear from the 60ish folks that they are concerned that they didn't start compounding their nest egg earlier. Given the previous 'Dirty Dozen' where they basically made no progress investing in the Market since the turn of the century, and the current low interest environment, they wonder if they have time to accumulate enough cash to allow them to retire within the next few years. The answer could lie in a special PPP with LIP that guarantees 6.25% to 7% compounded rate of return for income, offered by a handful of insurance companies.

Again, we'll use $100,000 as an initial deposit for the following illustration based on a 60 year old annuitant, deferring income for 10 years and taking joint income. Note that the company, in this example, opens the account with an 8% match (bonus) of the initial principal amount. The bonus is locked into the LIP from day one.

Year	Age	Benefit Base	Withdrawal %	Guaranteed Lifetime Withdrawal
0	60	$108,000	4.5%	**$4,860**
1	61	$115,560	4.6%	**$5,316**
2	62	$123,649	4.7%	**$5,812**
3	63	$132,305	4.8%	**$6,351**
4	64	$141,566	4.9%	**$6,937**
5	65	$151,476	5.0%	**$7,574**
6	66	$162,079	5.1%	**$8,266**
7	67	$173,424	5.2%	**$9,018**
8	68	$185,564	5.3%	**$9,835**
9	69	$198,554	5.4%	**$10,722**
10	**70**	**$212,452**	**5.5%**	**$11,685**
11	71	$227,324	5.6%	**$12,730**
12	72	$243,237	5.7%	**$13,864**
13	73	$260,263	5.8%	**$15,095**
14	74	$278,482	5.9%	**$16,430**
15	75	$297,975	6.0%	**$17,879**
16	76	$318,834	6.1%	**$19,449**
17	77	$341,152	6.2%	**$21,151**
18	78	$365,033	6.3%	**$22,997**
19	79	$390,585	6.4%	**$24,997**
20	80	$417,926	6.5%	**$27,165**
21	81	$417,926	6.6%	**$27,583**

Above, we show only the *Living* Benefit, not the Death Benefit. For details about how the Death Benefit works, contact your SWC, or submit a request on our website, www.RAFTstrategy.com.

Keep in mind that this special PPP with LIP is available in every State, yet it differs from State to State. Some states provide a *Match*; other States may have different bonus percentages or may not offer a bonus at all. Another feature often seen in this type of account is a *Healthcare Benefit*, which may double the payment to the annuitant for a period of years because of health reasons. Typically a health-care duplicator kicks in when a physician deems that the annuitant is unable to perform two of the six 'Activities of Daily Living' (ADLs) for a period of time; usually two or three months. The ADLs are defined as: feeding oneself, toileting, bathing oneself, transferring (i.e., moving from bed to wheelchair without assistance), dressing oneself, and incontinence.

Again, this is just an example. Your SWC can give you the tour according to the regulations in your State. With that said, notice the three most important features this PPP option offers:

1. Guaranteed high rate of compounding interest that determines a benefit base.
2. Tax-deferred growth for qualified or nonqualified options.
3. Permanent income that will last throughout the annuitant's life and provides an option for lifetime income for both spouses.

Most importantly, in order to determine the most effective PPP for you, consider whether you are concerned about leaving a legacy and how long your projected *time horizon* is. For some, starting a 10-year deferred income account at age 65 may be too late because they have major health issues and believe they will not have many years to use the income. For our super healthy friends, age 75 could still give them plenty of time to grow and use the LIP.

Often times, I meet with retirees who see the value in 'layering' their retirement nest egg by choosing to place some money in two or more PPP programs. For example, they may wish to fund one account, from which they plan to take 10% free withdrawals after the first anniversary date, and fund another account from which they plan to start taking distributions 5 or 10 year down the road.

I designed just such a program for a very savvy 70-year-young client of mine. She chose to place $100,000 into a LIP and allow it to compound for 6 years before taking income, which will provide her a guaranteed lifetime income in excess of $10,000 annually. She also chose to transfer another $150,000 from her IRA into a PPP IRA, which she will take 10% annually after her first year anniversary. The particular PPP we opened is designed to continue growing even as she is taking withdrawals. Keep in mind that at age 70 ½ she is compelled to take *Required Minimum Distributions* (RMDs) and pay the income tax, in order to avoid an IRS penalty. The 10% free withdrawals will more than cover her tax obligation and still leave her with around $10,000 a year to augment her Social Security payments, and provide her the income she needs to live on.

I shared ideas of how the PPP may work for those in their 50s, 60s, and 70s. Now let's talk about *Legacy Planning*. What can we recommend to retirees in their late 70s and early 80s? As I have stated already, products and companies vary widely. Typically the maximum age most insurance companies offer PPP programs for policyholders is 80 or 85.

I have an idea for you. In fact, the next illustration showcases a PPP I recommended to my own mother at age 72 and to my father-in-law at age 80 for two different reasons. Now, Grandpapa wanted to set aside $100,000 for his Grandkids. He felt he would not need to spend the money while he was living, so he just wanted a place to keep it. A place that would give him the principal guarantee and lock in gains every year. He also liked the 20% match which he considered the icing on the cake. We asked him, "How about a nice 20% bonus on all funds placed in PPP for the first 3 years?" He liked that and was all about turning his $100,000 investment into $120,000 day one. He is not planning on touching the account, so based on the 20 year look back, the 20% bonus, and the annual locked in gains, his account is projected to double in about 10 years. That is quite and nice legacy for his grandchildren. Now, provided he did need to access the money, he can take out 10% per year without any penalty and the account has NO FEES!

So what about Mom? How will she use the same PPP Program? A word about my Mother: She is a major Hero in my eyes. She gave birth to 11 happy, productive kids, which makes all of us look like underachievers. She is healthy as an ox and will likely live way past 100 years old. A few years back, she came to me for advice about one of her nest eggs of $50,000. I wanted to be sure she had it protected, yet could start living off the money while it was still growing. I showed her how to get the 20% bonus and still have access to her money.

We set up the PPP Program to start right around her birthday, so every year she is able to give herself a $5000 birthday gift. She takes 10% free withdrawals from her PPP annually. This particular account is designed to last 20 years. She will take 10% of her principal every year for the first 10 years, while it is still growing and compounding. (She skipped the first year because she didn't need it yet.) And after the 10th year, she will start withdrawing the rest of the principal, the interest based on the parameters and caps of the account. The 20% bonus plus interest enhancement, will also grow and compound and be locked in as new principal every year. Her PPP is projected to distribute something like this:

Age	Net Premiums	Credited interest	Accumulation Value	Value with Bonus	Withdrawals
72	$50,000				
73	$0	5.36%	$52,151	$62,846	$0
74	($5,000)	2.23%	$47,720	$58,718	$0
75	($5,000)	12.41%	$47,542	$60,234	$0
76	($5,000)	8.02%	$45,496	$59,433	$0
77	($5,000)	6.15%	$42,556	$57,518	$0

78	($5,000)	2.12%	$37,969	$53,297	$0
79	($5,000)	2.18%	$33,350	$49,057	$0
80	($5,000)	0.00%	$28,067	$43,774	$0
81	($5,000)	0.00%	$22,836	$38,543	$0
82	($5,000)	0.00%	$17,658	$33,365	$0
83		8.65%	$15,560	$32,770	$3,336
84		1.23%	$12,065	$29,499	$3,641
85		2.40%	$8,579	$26,460	$3,687
86		5.54%	$5,065	$24,021	$3,780
87		0.00%	$1,062	$20,018	$4,004
88		0.00%	$0	$16,014	$4,004
89		7.32%	$0	$12,933	$4,004
90		3.01%	$0	$8,895	$4,311
91		0.56%	$0	$4,474	$4,448
92		0.00%	$0		$4,474
Total	$5,000				$39,689

As I see it, Mom's account is projected to earn almost $35,000 interest (70% over the 20 years) even while she is accessing the funds along the way. I chose this particular PPP Program for her because she wanted to start using her money within the first few years. She did not want to defer the entire amount for several years, yet she does want it to last into her 90s. This is her 'mad money'. She uses it to travel, enjoy life, and have her Holiday. I determined her distributions are projected to be higher in this PPP than they would be with an income account.

Now you have some idea how the PPP can work for those opening the accounts in their 50s, 60s, 70s, and 80s. Still, we have just scratched the surface. I've said it many times before, yet it still bears repeating. Only a licensed SWC can help you determine which PPP Program will best suit your needs. We are here for you to provide that POM POM and help make 'Everyday a Holiday' for you!

Request an illustration from a qualified Strategic Wealth Coach through our website: www.RAFTStrategy.com.

Chapter 9

Third Jewel of the Triple Crown Solution: AAA (Asset Accumulation Access) Approach

I don't know why, but it seems that *three* is the magic number. I have been throwing around the term 'AAA Approach' for several years; and frankly, it has meant different things to me at different times. Throughout this entire effort of committing my thoughts to paper, I have pondered many times which approach I would showcase in this chapter and guess what? I still think they are all important to mention, so I am going to outline for you 3 AAA approaches to be used by individuals in 3 different financial situations, rich (let's say *everybody* is rich), richer, and richest:

1) Those looking for an additional predictable fixed income that will last as long as they do - the Longevity Insurance Protection (LIP)

2) Those who have assets like home equity that can be accessed to create additional streams of income and build an arbitrage using the RAFT

3) Those that have a substantial cash nest egg who do not feel they will spend all their money while they are living and want to leave a legacy.

Let's start out with the easy one, AAA approach #1, for the Rich: I have mentioned this before: It is the LIP. Why am I bridging the LIP from the PPP to the AAA? Because it is not only a PPP, but it is also a way to accumulate and access assets (AAA). I consider the LIP a hybrid between a PPP and the AAA because of the possibility to tap into the asset of the insurance company. Should you engage in the LIP and end up living a long time, thus spending all of your principal, and more interest than has accrued, you would truly be living off the insurance company's dime.

Because the LIP pays you for the rest of your life, even when your accumulation value has run dry, I would definitely say it is right for those who need and want the security of knowing they will always have money, no matter what. This AAA Crown Jewel ought to be a part of everyone's retirement solution because we can no longer count on Social Security and traditional pension plans to be there for us. How many times have we heard of companies that have decided they just cannot continue with the promise they initially made to their employees? How many times have we heard that Social Security is more like *Social Insecurity* because it may go broke? The LIP will bridge the gap and you can make the insurance company your retirement partner through this very special Asset Accumulation Access Approach.

AAA approach #2 for the Richer: Creating an arbitrage with your real estate assets.

I cannot tell you how many times listeners have called into the program conjecturing how they are going to pay off their home and be completely out to debt and therefore have POM POM. I get it! These folks have a stress button they think will magically disappear along with their mortgage. For some, who do not possess investor savvy or discipline, paying off their home may be their best solution. Yet, it does not mean it is the smartest decision. Now please don't get offended; follow me on this.

The may come as a surprise to you. . . I have been in debt before, too. In fact, 15 years ago, I was drowning in $100,000 of consumer debt. I know the feeling of debt burden. For me, I wanted to maintain a great credit rating, so I systematically paid it off over a 5 year period of time and it was torturous. I was so committed to getting out of debt, I thought of little else but muscling through it, day after day, depriving myself of luxuries and delaying gratification. It was tough, yet it was worth it. Today, I no longer have any debt, apart from my personal residence and investment properties.

At this point, my husband and I could pay off our homes with cash if we wanted to. Still, we resist because our mortgages are less than 4 % simple interest, and mortgage interest is still tax-deductible. At our tax bracket, 4% simple interest is more like 2.5% because we are able to deduct the interest from our income before we pay our taxes. Also, we know we can make at least an average of 8% compounded and tax-free in our RAFT account, which is about the same as gaining 12.5% taxable income.

Instead of paying off our homes, we have the discipline to take our money and invest it in PPP Programs and the RAFT Strategy, which historically have gained an average of 6-8% compounded return. We are more concerned with earning 6-8% compounded, rather than saving 2.5% simple interest by paying off our mortgage. Once you understand this concept, it is truly a no-brainer. Simple and compound interest are *not* the same, but if they were, and you had the choice to spend 2.5% in order to gain 7.5%, wouldn't you jump at the chance to create that 5% arbitrage? I would, and I do, all day long.

Smart people are not afraid to make money from OPM (Other People's Money). OPM could also mean the bank's money, like a tax-deductible mortgage. That is what I call 'good debt', (provided you have a decent rate.) There have been full books written on the subject of creating an arbitrage with your assets using inexpensive, low interest money to create a higher interest earning. For example, when you pay 3 % interest on a loan and place the money from the loan into an environment that earns 8%, you will create a surplus or arbitrage of 5%.

I just want to wake you up to the sheer genius and reality of good debt vs. bad debt. Bad debt, for example, could be consumer debt, like carrying credit card balances or car payments. Stay away from that! Pay off your credit card every month and avoid those crazy interest charges. As a teenager, I saw my parents struggle through a 16% second mortgage on their home. My Dad never wanted us kids to go through such pain. I remember him coaching me; he would always tell me to stay of the 'right side' of interest and debt. *"Earn interest, rather than Pay* interest," He would say, "Stay out of debt." It isn't always that simple, but there *is* such thing as 'Good Debt'. Good debt is borrowing money that will enable us to increase our assets or business beyond the cost of debt service.

So, next time you are tempted to pay off your home, ask yourself this question: "Am I too apathetic and/or ignorant to invest the money that I get for 3% into something where I can gain 6-8%?" If the answer is yes, then go ahead and pay off your home. Or, if you are just tired and don't want to think about it anymore, pay off your home. But, if the answer is **NO**, then start creating your tax-free and/or risk-free environment for retirement by using the RAFT Strategy and/or the PPP Program. With today's low interest rates, you may even consider separating equity from your home and placing it in a principal guaranteed growth account. Either way, consider taking the money you were going to throw at your home mortgage and invest it in to the RAFT or PPP instead. You will still have a tax deduction and the potential for a much higher increase, which mathematically is much better than saving 3-4% simple interest every year.

Do you want to know how my friend Rachel, who is 40, turned home equity into an AAA Approach? Well, she started by getting rid of her 6% mortgage which was left over from her refinance in 2004. Because she had a Freddie Mac loan, she qualified for the Federal Home Affordable Refinance Program (HARP) without having to skip house payments and trash her credit. (Fannie Mae loans also qualify for the HARP. Check with your lending institution to see which you have.) Anyway, Rachel contacted her lender to see if they would lower her rate using the HARP. They evaluated her excellent payment history and agreed to adjust her rate to from 6% to 3% fixed for 30 years. There were some closing costs, but they were rolled into the loan and much lower than they would have been, had she changed lenders.

I have been making this sound easy, but there were a few false starts. Because interest rates had dropped, Rachel had wanted to refinance for a few years. Unfortunately, her home equity had dropped as well. Does this sound familiar? She had applied for a refinance twice before, and was turned down because she has less than 20% equity. Rachel was frustrated because she saw her friends skipping payments and almost going into foreclosure only to be rescued by some government program. It did not seem fair that because she was diligently paying her mortgage on time, she was ignored and seemingly penalized for being responsible. I kept telling her to hang tough and keep trying. Finally, the HARP option opened up to those with good credit and she was treated with the respect she deserved. After a simple process which took a few months, her bank completed her new $300,000 loan at 3% interest for 30 years!

What did this new rate mean to Rachel? Well, instead of paying $18,000 a year in mortgage interest, she now pays only $9,000 in tax deductible interest. At her tax rate, she gets the real benefit of about $3000 in tax savings, so her home is truly only costing her roughly $6000/year in interest, or around $500/month. What did she decide to do with the $9,000/year she is saving because of the HARP? You might think the obvious strategy would be to put the additional $9,000/year towards paying off her home. And that was certainly an option. But think about it. As soon as she gives that money to the bank, she cannot get it back. It is locked into her home equity making 0% interest. Her home will increase or decrease in value, regardless how much equity she has. Yes, she would pay off her home in about half the time, but what would be the loss of investment opportunity cost her? How might she turn her HARP into an AAA?

You guessed it, she opened a RAFT. Using the RAFT keeps her money in a liquid position, so when she needs to help her kid with college tuition ten years down the road, she can tap into it. Instead of paying down her mortgage, she decided to take the $9000 she was saving every year and place it towards the RAFT Strategy for 20 years.

According to the illustration we provided for her, which we backed down to ½% below the average rate of return, Rachel will be insured for $713,000. The Death benefit would more than pay off her home should something happen to her. She would also be able to extract over $50,000/year from her RAFT starting at age 65.

You decide if she made the correct choice. By placing the $9000/year towards her mortgage, she would save roughly $150,000 in interest, but by placing the same amount towards her RAFT for 20 years, she could end up taking tax-free distribution of around $50,000 a year at age 65, for the rest of her life.

Let's say she lives to age 95; $50,000 x 30 years = $1.5 million in total tax-free distributions. If Rachel just makes it to age 85, thus living just 20 years into retirement, she would have extracted around a $1,000,000 from her RAFT and still have death benefit of $277,000 left for her survivors. To compare a similar illustration that shows proposed contributions, projected distributions, and relevant death benefit, go back to chapter 6. Keep in mind Rachel's total contributions are $180,000, whereas the illustrations provided in chapter 6 show total contributions of only $50,000 (less than ⅓ the amount of Rachel's contributions.)

Since the math is linear and the two policyholders are similar in age and health status, the annual distributions for Rachel's RAFT end up about 350% higher. See the following illustration:

Age	Year	Premium	Tax-Free Loans	Cumulative Net Outlay	Net Cash Value	Death Benefit
41	1	$9,000	$0	$9,000	$0	$713,656
42	2	$9,000	$0	$18,000	$0	$713,656
43	3	$9,000	$0	$27,000	$7,723	$713,656
44	4	$9,000	$0	$36,000	$17,093	$713,656
45	5	$9,000	$0	$45,000	$27,087	$713,656
46	6	$9,000	$0	$54,000	$37,830	$713,656
47	7	$9,000	$0	$63,000	$49,400	$713,656
48	8	$9,000	$0	$73,000	$61,865	$713,656
49	9	$9,000	$0	$81,000	$75,306	$713,656
50	10	$9,000	$0	$90,000	$89,832	$713,656
51	11	$9,000	$0	$99,000	$107,313	$713,656

52	12	$9,000	$0	$108,000	$126,086	$713,656
53	13	$9,000	$0	$117,000	$146,248	$713,656
54	14	$9,000	$0	$126,000	$167,902	$713,656
55	15	$9,000	$0	$135,000	$191,179	$713,656
56	16	$9,000	$0	$144,000	$216,189	$713,656
57	17	$9,000	$0	$153,000	$242,017	$713,656
58	18	$9,000	$0	$162,000	$269,875	$713,656
59	19	$9,000	$0	$171,000	$299,928	$713,656
60	20	$9,000	$0	$180,000	$332,354	$713,656
61	21	$0	$0	$180,000	$358,094	$713,656
62	22	$0	$0	$180,000	$385,841	$713,656
63	23	$0	$0	$180,000	$415,756	$713,656
64	24	$0	$0	$180,000	$448,015	$713,656
65	25	$0	$52,157	$180,000	$427,901	$658,735
66	26	$0	$52,157	$180,000	$407,652	$600,903
67	27	$0	$52,157	$180,000	$387,389	$540,005
68	28	$0	$52,157	$180,000	$367,245	$476,148
69	29	$0	$52,157	$180,000	$347,377	$458,332
70	30	$0	$52,157	$180,000	$327,688	$440,342
71	31	$0	$52,157	$180,000	$308,243	$422,170
72	32	$0	$52,157	$180,000	$289,222	$395,735
73	33	$0	$52,157	$180,000	$270,790	$368,021
74	34	$0	$52,157	$180,000	$253,135	$338,966
75	35	$0	$52,157	$180,000	$236,480	$308,516
76	36	$0	$52,157	$180,000	$221,092	$276,623

77	37	$0	$52,157	$180,000	$206,949	$266,876
78	38	$0	$52,157	$180,000	$194,259	$258,925
79	39	$0	$52,157	$180,000	$183,249	$253,023
80	40	$0	$52,157	$180,000	$174,170	$249,449
81	41	$0	$52,157	$180,000	$167,281	$248,490
82	42	$0	$52,157	$180,000	$162,852	$250,446
83	43	$0	$52,157	$180,000	$161,182	$255,649
84	44	$0	$52,157	$180,000	$162,592	$264,456
85	45	$0	$52,157	$180,000	$167,419	$277,238
Total			**$1,074,297**			

Bottom line, in Rachel's situation, she could save $150,000 in interest over a 20 year period of time by paying off her home. Or, she could have the potential tax-free distributions of million dollars or more. I believe she maximized the AAA approach by making the right choice to fund her RAFT.

So, there you have it; the AAA Approach for handling your home equity. There is so much more that could be explored for AAA Approach #2, but just remember the difference between good debt and bad debt. As in the New Testament, the parable of the talents showcases the foolish servant who buried his money so as not to lose it. The wise servant showed he was responsible with the money because he invested and multiplied it. That is what AAA is all about; being a wise steward of the money and assets entrusted to you.

Most anyone with a bit of a nest egg can engage in the 'rich' AAA Approach using the LIP. Those who own a home may be able to manage the 'richer' AAA Approach for Home Equity. Even fewer are able to use the 'richest' AAA because it can only be achieved with money that is purposefully to be left to legacy. So let's see if AAA Approach #3 is for you.

AAA Approach #3 for the Richest: Using the Stretch IRA to minimize tax burden for you and your legacy.

This final AAA Approach I will describe is truly for those who cannot possibly spend all the money they have while they are still living and they do not want to relegate their beneficiaries to paying high taxes because they have left a giant lump sum legacy. This strategy is for those of you with an IRA because we are going to share with you how to minimize the tax burden from your IRA while maximizing your tax-deferred distributions.

There are a handful of insurance companies that offer Stretch-Friendly annuities that can be used to *stretch* your assets throughout your lifetime, through the next generation, and perhaps beyond. Because the income stream from such an account is based IRS guidelines for Required Minimum Distributions (RMDs) and life expectancy, the tax burden is typically much less than it would be for that of willing a lump sum to your beneficiary. Let me explain.

The AAA Approach, Stretch strategy, is an estate-planning option designed to continue your investment plan for the next generation. It can extend the tax-deferred earning power of your PPP, which would be an IRA or non-qualified annuity. It can produce a lifetime income stream that spreads out the tax liability for your beneficiaries. When you pass away, your PPP may be transferred to your spouse so the investment can continue accumulating. When your spouse passes away, the account is passed on to the beneficiaries who can also choose to Stretch the IRA or non-qualified annuity. Keep in mind that the whole system could fall apart, unless your spouse restricts the payout to your beneficiary, because your spouse's beneficiary would have access to more than just the RMD.

You have a choice in structuring your Stretch. You can educate your beneficiaries and leave it to them to decide how they want to follow through. Or, you can set up an involuntary, predetermined Stretch process that must be followed upon your death. Should you choose the involuntary payout, the insurance company with which you work can design and restricted distributions adhering to IRS guidelines. Your money could provide a steady stream of income for your progeny to pay for education, start businesses, buy homes, or any number of important events. Using this Stretch AAA Approach could ensure that your legacy plan benefits your spouse, your children, and even your grandchildren.

You can easily access Stretch calculators on the internet and plug in the numbers that make sense for you. Yet, implementing the strategy is where you want to contact a professional, because it is important to set it up according to IRS guidelines. Check out the following Stretch calculations.

Based on a $500,000 IRA and an average RoR of 4%, below is an example of how the Stretch can work for a 70 year old couple who wants to leave this AAA Legacy for their grandchild:

Total Distributions

- Total projected distributions during owner's lifetime:	$241,782.77
- Total projected distributions during surviving spouse's lifetime:	$298,509.09
- Total projected distributions during spouse's beneficiary's lifetime:	<u>$942,870.32</u>
- Total projected distributions:	$1,483,162.18

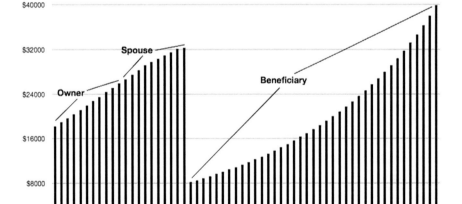

Account Balances and Minimum Distributions by Year

Note how these loving grandparents were able to turn $500,000 into almost $1.5 Million of distributions over their lifetimes and the lifetime of their grandchild by using the Stretch strategy. By taking only the IRS required RMDs, they minimized the tax burden along the way, while providing a substantial income stream for two or more generations.

I hope you these AAA Approaches expanded your thinking about accessing your assets in the most beneficial ways. Every individual's situation is unique, so don't be shy, get advice. We look forward to hearing from you and helping you implement the entire Triple Crown Solution.

AAA Summary

Three Smart AAA Approaches:
-Annuities with income riders: Longevity Insurance Protection
-Harvesting home equity to fund the RAFT Strategy, PPP, or a LIP
-Using RMDs for maximum legacy distributions through Stretch IRA and non-qualified annuities.

To receive advice concerning which AAA Approach(es) you might apply to your retirement nest egg, contact a qualified SWA through our website: www.RAFTstrategy.com

Chapter 10

The Triple Crown Solution at Work:

One of my earliest memories is peering over the top over the top of the dinner table to see my birthday cake as I turned 3 years old. I remember Mom sitting me on top of a stack of three telephone books, so I would be tall enough to blow out my candles. Just beyond the candlelight stood my handsome Dad, in full military uniform. That was almost 50 years ago and it seems like yesterday. Now I'm attending my *Grandchildren's birthday* parties and I marvel how the years fly by faster as I age.

What happened to all that time? Maybe you feel somewhat the way I do. How did those kids grow up so fast and start having kids of their own? Did I raise them right? Am I living the future I planned? You might ask yourself this: "Was I able to put away what I should have for retirement? Is my money going to last as long as I do?" There is so much life to live and so little time; it is a wonder we are able to accomplish a fraction of our desires. Nobody should have to make every decision on their own or do everything by themselves. I find those who are humble enough to ask others for advice and assistance tend to move to the front of the achievers line of life.

You have access to the tools to build a RAFT, pursue the PPP and engage in the AAA. Now you must seek the knowledge of a trained and qualified SWC. They will help you put it all together.

In my role of SWC I sometimes feel like I'm on the Price is Right because I am asked the same questions over and over. So ala game show style, I'm going to give you the answers to the top questions behind door number 1, 2, and 3:

Top Question behind Door Number 1: Laurett, you recommend working with a variety of insurance companies. What is risk of any of those companies going under?

According to the Business and Finance section of Wikipedia, there are over 2000 companies offering life insurance in the US and collectively the own, manage, and control more assets than all the banks in the World combined. These companies reportedly also own, manage, and control more assets than all the oil companies in the World combined. If one company has to close their doors, there are 1,999 other insurance companies poised to service the displaced policyholders' accounts. By law, these companies must adhere to the parameters of each policyholder's contract.

During the great depression, it was the insurance companies that bailed out the banks, not the Federal Government. So you might ask, "What happened to AIG a few years back when the Feds had to step in a bail them out?" Well, AIG had experienced worldwide losses, especially in the mortgage-backed security arena and they needed a boost to get out of the pickle they were in. The good news is that by law, insurance companies are obligated to set aside enough reserves to meet their annual financial responsibilities to the policyholders. According to actuarial formulas, insurance companies have a pretty sound idea how many policyholders will pass in this year. They know how many assets they will need to pay the beneficiaries and annuitants, in order to meet all of their financial obligations.

Policyholders are also protected on another level; by their State Guarantee Fund (SGF). Similar to the way FDIC secures bank accounts, The SGF insures annuities and life policies. Coverage differs from State to State, but most SGFs cover each account up to $300,000 and some cover up to $500,000. Insurance companies are not allowed to tap into the protected assets that are secured by the SGF. Had AIG been able to do so, they may not have needed the Government bailout after all. And still, look what happened with AIG. They were able to pay back the Federal loan. . . plus over $23 billion interest in just a few years. Bam! These insurance companies are solid!

With that said, insurance companies are graded by rating agencies like Standard & Poor's, A.M. Best, and Moody's in terms of financial strength and solvency, just like other businesses. There are so many top rated insurance companies in the US, it is easy to find A and AA rated companies with which to set up your RAFT or PPP. With all these safe guards in place, I cannot think of a better financial institution in which to invest your money than a top rated insurance company.

- Top Question behind Door Number 2: I understand the tax benefits of the RAFT and the PPP as of today; but what are the chances the IRS will change the rules?

Well, the IRS can pretty much do whatever they want. They can nix the whole idea of TEFRA, DEFRA and TAMRA. They could do away with section 101 and provisions 7702, 72 (e), 72(t) and 72(q) at any time and that would create a whole boatload of unhappy RAFTers. Yet, I truly believe that will *not* happen anytime soon. Every year, the insurance industry lobbies to continue these very special tax treatments for retirement funds and every year they remain approved.

We understand that you want to place your nest egg in a risk-free and preferably a tax-free *environment for retirement*. Once started, you don't want to have to unwind it because the IRS had dropped the tax-advantaged status. That's where 'Grandfathering' comes in. Grandfathering means that whatever laws were in place when a tax strategy was used, those laws will always govern that particular tax treatment. Even if the law changes, it will only affect accounts that were started after the change was made. The original laws would continue to govern any tax treatment that pre-dates the change.

The IRS is constantly revising the tax code, so one of the ways they keep peace with those affected by the changes is to Grandfather the tax-treatment according to the date a certain strategy was implemented. Bottom line; if you are the least bit concerned that the RAFT Strategy will no longer be accepted by the IRS, get your account open now, before the tax laws change.

With that in mind, there are many ways to craft the RAFT. As long as the policy owner qualifies from a health standpoint, we can show them any number of funding options. For example, one option that truly appeals to business owners and medical practitioners is to set up the RAFT to accept a future lump sum payment, without causing a MEC. To ensure our clients are able to take full advantage of the RAFT strategy, we often assist business owners and professionals who will one day sell their business, firm, or practice. We may coach them to set up the RAFT account initially for minimal funded while they are still working and to accept a large lump sum from the sale of their business, once they retire. The goal is to 'dump the lump' into the RAFT because it can then continue to grow and be accessed tax-free.

An SWC can help set up this special RAFT by increasing the death benefit according to IRS guidelines and instructing the policy owner to under fund the account for several years. For example, provided we want to ultimately place a million dollars into the RAFT because we believe the business will sell for $500,000. We might set it up to accept $100,000 a year for 10 years, but only fund it at $50,000/year. So, ten year down the road, when the business is sold, we have only placed $500,000 into the bucket that is ready to accept $1,000,000. We can then place the $500,000 from the sale of the business in one lump sum without causing it to become a MEC* and therefore preserving the tax-free status.

*A word about Modified Endowment Contracts:

Before we move on to the last question, I want to mention that even though this book has been largely dedicated to explaining how to create a tax-free environment for retirement, I believe using MECs for retirement purposes can be appropriate for some. As there are many ways to set up a RAFT, there are also many ways to set up a MEC. Given that the money earned in a MEC is taxable at ordinary income tax rates, why would anyone want a MEC? Because some insurance companies provide a few features in a MEC that may make it an attractive option for the short term investor or someone who wants to place a large sum of money, without being tied to adhering to the 7-pay rule of a properly designed and funded RAFT. I suggest looking for the following benefits:

1. 0% loan option after 5 years, (most EIULs offer 0% loans only after 10 Years of ownership)
2. Indexed allocations with multiple crediting options from which to choose
3. By choosing Waiver of Surrender option, no surrender charges for withdrawing cash value. (Withdrawals will be taxed at regular income tax rates.)
4. Optional Long Term Care (LTC) Benefit Rider can be purchased at the time of issue. Typically, an LTC benefit can be activated when a medical professional deems the policyholder is unable to perform at least 2 of the 6 ADLs for 90 days. Some insurance companies offer an LTC benefit of up to 24% of the death benefit annually for up to 4 years. For example, if the death benefit is $1 million, the LTC would provide up to $20,000/month to the insured, which would be as much as $240,000 a year. Companies typically have a maximum LTC benefit and payout. Be sure to check the maximum annual and lifetime benefit offered.
5. Note that LTC benefit distributions are **tax-free** and subtracted from the death benefit.
6. Apart from the mortality costs and policy expenses, funds within a MEC are 100% liquid from day one.
7. According to current IRS guidelines, the death benefit from any insurance policy to its beneficiaries, including a death benefit from a MEC, is 100% income **tax-free**.

As long as the potential policyholder is insurable at standard rates or better, he or she will have the choice to set up a RAFT or a MEC. Many of our clients, particularly those who are over age 60 opt for the MEC because they can fund it faster than the RAFT and may want to have instant liquidity without being subject to surrender charges. A MEC may be a sensible option for you if you are not too concerned with accessing your interest return tax-free while you are living.

We answered the questions about insurance companies and the IRS changing the rules, so let's see what question lies behind the final door.

- Top Question behind Door Number 3: I like all three Jewels of the Triple Crown Solution; yet what if I set up one of those accounts and I change my mind after the first year?

Do you remember in Chapter 6 when we discussed the *Smart* way, the *Dumb* way, and the *Sad* way to access your money from your life insurance policy? The Sad way is to die, the Smart way is borrow it out against the face amount and because of the penalties and tax consequences, and the dumb way is to *surrender* the policy. So, I would say that if you are not quite sure you want to follow through with these long term strategies of the Triple Crown Solution, you probably ought to not even start.

Ways to Get Money Out of the R.A.F.T.

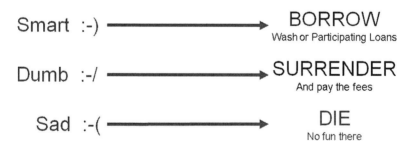

Smart :-) ⟶ BORROW
Wash or Participating Loans

Dumb :-/ ⟶ SURRENDER
And pay the fees

Sad :-(⟶ DIE
No fun there

There you have it; the answers to the most commonly asked questions. The Price IS Right! It costs you nothing but your time to set up these options. You have just won the opportunity to engage in the Triple Crown Solution.

We recognize that not all these strategies are appropriate for every person and that each concept is best utilized as part of an overall retirement plan. For example, the PPP would not suitable for an individual that intends to take a large lump sum out of his or her account during the first few years of ownership because there may be surrender charges on a portion of the withdrawal. (But a MEC or RAFT might be suitable.) Taking out a large lump sum cannibalizes the potential returns and defeats the purpose of creating the future income stream.

A MEC may not appropriate for someone who wants a tax-free living benefit, and RAFT may not work for someone who does not have a long enough time horizon to allow it to grow before taking distributions. Building retirement security is tricky, yet simple. You just need the right information for YOU.

Remember also, that Zero is Hero when it comes to the Triple Crown Solution. There are Zero Fees to pay in most of the PPP Programs we endorse. Zero loss when the markets dive. Zero % interest on tax-free distributions, and ZERO time to lose in setting up your future.

If you think you are too old to engage in the concepts you have read about in this book, pass this information to those who aren't, like your children or grandkids, and ask an SWC for their advice.

If you think you don't have enough money to get started on anything, ask an SWC for their advice.

If you think you are too young, too inexperienced, too smart, or too tough, whatever you think. . .just stop and call us to ask an SWC for their advice.

Why do you think we are teaching people how to take charge of their life and their retirement?

According to the Pew Research Center, just over a quarter of the total U.S. population is "baby boomers," which refers to the dramatic post–World War II baby boom from 1946 to 1964. I am one of this 26% preparing for retirement, and I realize that I am facing very different circumstances than my parents did. My children are in an even more challenging situation.

Because we are all projected to live longer than did our parents or grandparent, we are going to have many more years in retirement and if we are not prepared, we may not be able to retire at all. I see many elderly folks working jobs these days. I'm hoping, for the most part, they are working because they enjoy the interaction. But I'm guessing there are many out there working because they need the money. Social *Insecurity*

Just isn't cutting it and many no longer have the pensions they thought they would.

Check out the following chart to see how far your life expectancy might take you. Are you a guy, a gal, single or part of a couple? As you can see, if you have already reached a certain age, you have 25% or 50 % chance to live even longer. Provided you are one of the lucky ones who lives into their 90s and beyond, will you have enough money to last as long as you do?

Longer Life Expectancies

It's good news that life expectancy is increasing by 2 months every year - but we have to be prepared for it!

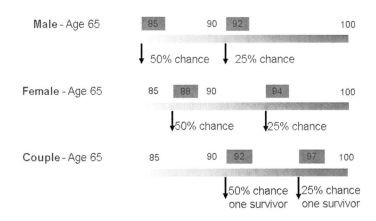

If you've listened to Freedom Financial Radio Network, you have likely heard us speak of retirement planning as a three or four legged stool. Most of us hope Social Security will be one leg on the 'retirement stool'. Maybe a pension would be another leg, and then we are on our own. In order for our stool to stand on its own, we need at least 3 legs. How many legs do you have on your retirement stool? Might it be nice to add a RAFT leg and a PPP leg as well? Four legged stools are pretty stable.

Heaven forbid if you have not built a retirement stool at all. What if you were just sitting on a tree stump at the end of your working years, like the character in Shel Silverstein's book *The Giving Tree*? Stumps can be stable too, as long as they have deep roots. How deep are your roots? Is your stump going to crumble because of a termite infestation of taxes and inflation? Is it going to rot from the stormy weather of the *SHOCK* market? The education you have received through reading this book has caused your roots to dig deeper because you now KNOW what you need to do. Don't miss out on the opportunity to follow through.

I'm giving you a chance to believe in your future; to engage in some sound strategies that have stood the test of time. Are you ready to dig those roots down deep so they can reach the spring waters of prosperity? Only trees with deep roots grow large and weather the storms. You have a choice. You can take the seeds that have been planted in you as you have read this book and you can seek the proper sunshine of advice from a SWC who can recommend the suitable solutions for you and grow a large tree for your nest egg. Or, you can keep chopping those little seedlings' roots by experiencing the losses in the Market and limiting your growth. I call that 'The Bonsai Effect' because every time we cut the roots, it limits the growth of the tree.

Your investments will only grow to their full potential if we place them in fertile ground where they won't continue to be cut off at the roots. And YOU will only grow to your full potential as you absorb and implement the sound principles you learn every day. I pray you will explore how the concepts of the Triple Crown Solution may work for you, like they have for thousands of other successful individuals. As you go through this journey of financial discovery, we are here to guide you.

As we say each week on the radio, "Have a great week and God Bless." Well, you have just finished reading *The RAFT Strategy: How to build your Tax-Free Nest Egg Without Risk*, so I want to congratulate you and take it a step further by saying, "Have a great LIFE and God Bless!"

To contact a Strategic Wealth Coach in your area, go to
our website:
www.RAFTstrategy.com

~Epilogue~

What do I do now?

I s anyone out there as annoyed as I am with the *lack of change* the White House has brought to the table over the past 4+ years? Come on. . . the National deficit has gone from 10.6 Trillion to over 17 Trillion on Obama's watch and for every dollar we borrow, about 28 cents goes straight to line the silk pockets of China and other foreign investors. Gas prices have doubled since 2008 and are still over $4.00/gallon, 8 months after the 2012 election. The Bureau of Labor Statistics reports that the unemployment rate is still hovering just below 8%, which, BTW, does not include those who have given up looking for a job. Many experts project the real unemployment figure at around 18%.

Our children are not growing up in the same Country we enjoyed. For the first time ever in the history of America the next generation is less prosperous than the last. At the cost of about $134/month per person, almost 50 million Americans are engaged in the Supplemental Nutrition Subsistence Program (SNAP), aka food stamps. Roughly 15 % of our population, or one in six contribute to the $6.025 billion spent every month on SNAP. What's that expression? "Oh, SNAP!"

Higher education costs are out of control. In fact, according to Bloomberg, the cost of living has increased by 115% since 1986 and yet the average college tuition has increased almost 500%. An education that cost $10,000/year in 1986 has gone up to $59,000/year, not to the $21,000 that would be expected had higher learning costs simply kept pace with inflation. Millions of students are exiting Universities with a non-cancellable mortgage of student loan debt. The cumulative student loans in America are now higher than the National total of credit card debt, at over $1 trillion.

Tax rates are up and expected to continue climbing. Most can see that economically, politically and even socially, our World is in chaos. The United States cannot continue down this road and still be the great, powerful watchdog nation it has always been. The burden of financial correction lies on each of us to make the solid decisions that will impact the lives of our families for generations to come. What are you going to do to guard against higher taxes, inflation, and the volatility of the Market?

This is your life, your retirement, your future. Don't expect government programs to bail you out, because they can barely take care of themselves. Take charge now and do what it takes to perpetuate, preserve, and protect your assets. Five, ten or twenty years from now I don't want to hear you say, "I wish I had." I want to hear that you are looking back at the time you read _The RAFT Strategy: How to Build Your Tax-Free Nest Egg Without Risk_ and you say to yourself, "I took Laurett's advice. . . and I'm glad I did."

Glossary

101, Section of the IRC - (see **Internal Revenue Code, Section 101**)

1035, Section of the IRC - (see **Internal Revenue Code, Section 1035**)

401(k) plan - A qualified retirement plan set up by employers that allows employees to make pre-tax contributions from their salary. The employer may also make matching contributions to the plan on the employee's behalf. Earnings on a 401(k) accrues tax-deferred. Roth 401(k) plan are funded with after-tax money.

403(b) plan - A retirement plan for certain employees of public schools, tax-exempt organizations and certain ministers. Similar to the 401(k), the employee makes regular salary deferral contributions. Also known as a tax-sheltered annuity (TSA) plan. Individual 403(b) Plans can be in the form of an annuity contract provided through an insurance company, a custodial account which is invested in mutual funds, or a retirement income account set up for church employees.

457 plan - A non-qualified plan set up by state and local governments, tax-exempt governments, and tax-exempt employers. Employees make salary deferral contributions. Earnings accrue on a tax-deferred basis and contributions are not taxed until the assets are distributed from the plan.

7-Pay Test - Test used to determine if an insurance policy is a Modified Endowment Contract (MEC). It is a limitation on the total amount you can pay into your policy in the first seven years of its existence. IRC states, "A contract fails to meet the 7-pay test of this subsection if the accumulated amount paid under the contract at any time during the 1st 7 contract years exceeds the sum of the net level premiums which would have been paid on or before such time if the contract provided for paid-up future benefits after the payment of 7 level annual premiums"

72(t), IRS Rule - An Internal Revenue Service (IRS) rule that allows an individual to withdraw funds from an IRA account without penalty as long as the IRA owner takes at least five substantially equal periodic payments (SEPPs). The payment amount is determined by the IRA owner's life expectancy, as calculated with various IRS-approved methods.

7702, Section of the IRC - (see **Internal Revenue Code, Section 7702**)

AAA - The highest possible rating assigned to an insurance policy by credit rating agencies. It is considered having little risk of default and an exceptional degree of creditworthiness.

'AAA' – Acronym for Asset Accumulation Access, coined by the Author

accumulation value - (see **cash value**)

actuarial formulas - Formulas or assumptions used to determine the premiums charged on a life or health insurance policies. These formulas ensure sufficient coverage of potential medical costs or death benefit and align insurance company solvency with projected outlay for benefits.

actuary - A professional statistician that works for a/n (insurance) company who mathematically evaluates the probability of events and qualifies contingent outcomes in order to minimize financial loss and ensure company solvency.

adjusted gross income (AGI) - A measure of income used to determine how much of your income is taxable. It is calculated as your gross income from taxable sources minus allowable deductions, such as unreimbursed business expenses, medical expenses, alimony and deductible retirement plan contributions. Also known as 'net income'.

Activities of Daily Living (ADLs) Six everyday functions individuals are able to perform in order to be deemed in good physical health by a medical professional. The ADLs are: dressing, feeding, bathing oneself, transferring (for example, moving from bed to wheelchair), toileting, and incontinence.

annuity - A financial product or account that pays annually. Annuities are primarily used in retirement planning to enable a person to preserve and grow funds.

AGI - (see **adjusted gross income**)

baby boomers - Generation of people born between 1946 and 1964. Baby boomers make up nearly 20% of the U.S. population and therefore have a significant impact on the economy. Baby boomers are largely entering or will soon enter the retirement phase of their lives.

Barclays Capital Aggregate Bond - A market capitalization-weighted index (i.e., the securities in the index are weighted according to the market size of each bond type) that is often used to represent investment grade bonds being traded in the United States and maintained by Barclays Capital.

basis – The original amount of an investment, before interest has accrued.

bear market - A condition of the stock market when prices of securities are falling, and investors are largely pessimistic. Investors may sell as they anticipate losses, which may perpetuate the pessimism and continuation of the bear market.

beneficiary - Person named as the recipient of distributions from a life insurance policy, trust, or will; following the death of the policy, asset, or property owner.

bond - A fixed-income security in which an investor loans money to a corporate or government agency and receives interest from that loan at a later date. The amount of interest is determined by the credit quality of the bond and its maturity date, which can be anywhere from 90 days to 30 years. Interest is usually paid every six months.

burn rate - The rate at which a new company spends its venture capital before generating a positive cash flow. It is generally quoted in terms of how much cash is spent per month.

Bush Tax Cuts - A series of temporary income tax relief measures enacted by President George W. Bush in 2001 and 2003. The tax cuts lowered federal income tax rates for everyone, decreased the marriage penalty, lowered capital gains taxes, lowered the tax rate on dividend income, increased the child tax credit from $500 to $1,000 per child, eliminated the phaseout of personal exemptions for higher-income taxpayers and eliminated the phaseout of itemized deductions and eliminated the estate tax.

calls - A form of stock option. Calls increase in value when the security is going up, and decrease in value when the price of the security declines. A call option allows an individual to buy stock from the investor it was purchased from at a specific price on or before a specific date. See **puts**.

capital gain - The increase in value of an investment or real estate that results in a higher worth than the original purchase price. The gain is determined when the asset is sold, and must be claimed on income taxes.

capital gains tax - The tax levied on the profits (capital gains) of an asset after it is sold.

cash value - The amount of money an insurance company will pay to the policyholder or annuity holder when the policy is voluntarily terminated before its maturity or the insured event occurs. Also known as 'accumulation value', 'surrender value', 'cash surrender value', and 'policyholder's equity'.

CD - (see **certificate of deposit**)

certificate of deposit - A promissory note or savings certificate issued by a bank. The owner of the CD receives interest after the CD matures, which can range from one month to five years. There is a penalty to withdrawing funds before the maturity date.

compound interest - The amount of interest that is added to the initial principal of a deposit, loan or debt. Compounding interest allows the principal to grow faster than simple interest. It is generally calculated on an annual basis. It can be referred to as compounded growth.

compounded growth - (see **compound interest**)

Consumer Price Index (CPI) - A measure of the weighted average of prices of a certain group of consumer goods, such as transportation, food and medical care. The CPI is calculated by averaging the price changes of the products and weighting them according to their importance. The CPI is one of the most frequently used statistical resources in identifying periods of inflation and deflation.

cost of living - The amount of money needed to meet basic living expenses such as housing, food, taxes and medical expenses. Cost of living is often used when comparing how expensive it is in one city compared to another.

CPI - (see **Consumer Price Index**)

CSO table, 2001 - The 2001 CSO Mortality Tables represent the most widely used approximations as to the expected rates of death in the United States as a function of age. Developed by the American Academy of Actuaries, it is included in the Academy's Commissioners Standard Ordinary Task Force final report of 2001. To see report, go to http://www.actuary.org/content/cso-task-force-report

DALBAR - A leading financial research organization. DALBAR develops standards for, and provides research, ratings, and rankings of intangible factors to the mutual fund, broker/dealer, discount brokerage, life insurance, and banking industries. See www.dalbar.com

death benefit - The amount of money a beneficiary receives from an insurance policy upon the death of the insured.

Deficit Reduction Act of 1984 (DEFRA) - DEFRA is an IRS guideline that modified the TEFRA rules of 1982, providing a general set of qualifications for any contract to qualify as a life insurance policy for income tax purposes.

DEFRA - (see **Deficit Reduction Act of 1984**)

dividend - A distribution of a certain amount of a company's earnings to its stockholders. Also, mandatory distribution of income and realized capital gains made to mutual fund, and other types of investors.

dot com - Refers to .com, or the top-level domain used by the Internet's Domain Naming System. A dot com company is one that does most of its business online. The dot com bubble refers to the financial period running from 1995 to 2001.

DOW - (see **Dow Jones Industrial Average**)

Dow Jones Industrial Average (DOW) - A price-weighted average of 30 significant stocks traded on the New York Stock Exchange and the Nasdaq. When the TV networks say "the market is up today," they are generally referring to the Dow.

EBRI - (see **Employee Benefits Research Institute**)

EIA - (see **Equity Indexed Annuity**)

EIUL - (see **Equity Indexed Universal Life insurance policy**)

Employee Benefits Research Institute (EBRI) - A nonpartisan nonprofit research agency. Research is conducted on health, savings, retirement, and economic securities issues. The EBRI is a reputable and quotable agency.

equity - The amount of ownership in any asset after all debt associated with that asset is deducted.

Equity Indexed Annuity (EIA) - A type of tax-deferred annuity linked to the growth of an equity index, typically the S&P 500, Nasdaq, Dow or an international index. It is a more conservative type of investment as it guarantees a minimum interest rate and protects against a loss in principal. Also known as an Indexed Annuity.

Equity Indexed Universal Life insurance policy (EIUL) - A permanent life insurance policy that allows policyholders to tie accumulation values to a stock market index. Indexed universal life insurance policies typically contain a minimum guaranteed fixed interest rate component along with indexed returns.

Ernst and Young – One of the largest privately held accounting firms in the World (part of the "Big Four" accounting firms, along with Deloitte, KPMG, and Price Waterhouse Cooper). It is headquartered in London, England and has employees in over 140 countries.

FA - (see **fixed annuity**)

FDIC - (see **Federal Deposit Insurance Corporation**)

federal deficit - The total amount of money that the United States owes its creditors. Also referred to as the Federal debt.

Federal Deposit Insurance Corporation (FDIC) - A corporation based in the United States that protects U.S. banks against failure and guarantees individual bank accounts against loss due to bank failure or robbery, up to a certain amount per account.

FIA - Fixed Indexed Annuity

Financial Times Stock Exchange (FTSE) - A company that specializes in index calculation. Although not part of a stock exchange, co-owners include the London Stock Exchange and the *Financial Times*. The FTSE is similar to Standard & Poor's in the United States. They are best known for the FTSE 100. http://ftse.com

Financial Times Stock Exchange 100 (FTSE 100) - An index of the top 100 blue-chip stocks on the London Stock Exchange.

First in, First out (FIFO) - An asset-management and valuation method in which the assets produced or acquired first are sold, used or disposed of first. For example, in the case of annuities, taxes are assessed FIFO meaning that tax would be paid on the principal first and the interest later.

fixed annuity (FA) - An insurance product in which the insurance company guarantees a fixed distribution annually from the contract. Earnings grow tax-deferred.

fixed indexed annuity (FIA) - An insurance product that provides the principal guarantee of fixed annuities combined with earning interest credits based on linking the money within the account to an external market index – without directly participating in the market.

fixed-rate - When referring to interest, it is the amount of interest on a loan, mortgage, or other liability that remains the same, or fixed, for the entire term of the liability, or part of the term.

Fortune 500 - An annual list of the five hundred most profitable US industrial corporations.

Freedom Financial Radio Network (FFRN) (1) - A radio network that airs Freedom Talk Radio, hosted by the Author, in several cities across the nation. FFRN connects life insurance professionals with listeners to the radio program for advice and information on tax-free retirement strategies. http://freedomfinancialradio.com/

FTSE - (see **Financial Times Stock Exchange**)

FTSE 100 - (see **Financial Times Stock Exchange 100**)

Gallop Poll - A division of Gallup, Inc. (a U.S. based company that provides data driven news) that regularly conducts public opinion polls in the U.S. and over 140 countries. http://gallup.com

grade corporate bonds (3) - Bonds that have a relatively low risk of default.

Great Depression - A severe economic depression that had world-wide effects in the decade prior to World War II. It began with the Wall Street Crash of October, 1929. It was characterized by high unemployment, poverty, low profits, deflation, and overall lack of confidence in the economic future.

HERO'S Talk Radio - Radio program(s) hosted by Laurett Ellsworth and/or Dave Arenz. HERO'S in an acronym for Health, Education,

Relationships and Opportunities as balanced by Spirituality. www. herostrategies.com

housing crisis of 2008 - Also known as subprime mortgage crisis. This crisis occurred due to a rise in subprime (making loans to people who have difficulty meeting payments) mortgage delinquencies and foreclosures, and the resulting decline of securities backed by these mortgages. Several major financial institutions collapsed in September 2008, which caused a significant disruption in the flow of credit to businesses and consumers and the onset of a severe global recession.

income tax - A tax assessed to individuals and businesses based on the income earned. Payment is made to the State or Federal government. The amount of income tax paid depends on many factors including amount earned, number of dependents, business expenses and losses, etc.

Individual Retirement Account (IRA) – A tax-deferred investment tool used to set aside money for retirement. Types of IRA's include Traditional IRAs, Roth IRAs, SIMPLE IRAs and SEP IRAs.

inflation - The balance at which the prices of goods and services is rising while purchasing power is falling.

Initial Public Offering (IPO) - The first sale of stock by a private company to the public.

IPO - (see **Initial Public Offering**)

IRC - (see **Internal Revenue Code**)

IRA - (see **Individual Retirement Account**)

IRS - (see **Internal Revenue Service**)

IRS code - alternate name for **IRC** (see **Internal Revenue Code**)

income rider - It is a type of living or death benefit added to a life insurance policy or annuity that provides the owner or annuitant income for the rest of his or her live and/or income for beneficiaries for a certain period of time.

indexes - Plural of index. An index is a statistical measure of change in an economy or securities market. The Standards & Poor 500 is one of the world's most often used indexes. Other prominent indexes include the DJ Wilshire 5000 (total stock market), the MSCI EAFE (foreign stocks in Europe, Australasia, Far East) and the Lehman Brothers Aggregate Bond Index (total bond market).

Internal Revenue Code (IRC) - The complex and inclusive set of tax laws created by the Internal Revenue Service (IRS). Federal tax law begins with the Internal Revenue Code (IRC), enacted by Congress in Title 26 of the United States Code (26 U.S.C.).

Section 101 - defines tax rules related to death benefits of life insurance contracts; located in Chapter 1 of Title 26 of the U.S.C.

Section 1035 - defines rules concerning gains and losses involved in exchanges of insurance policies; located in Chapter 1 of Title 26 of the

Section 7702A - defines a Modified Endowment Contract (MEC); a contract is an MEC if it is a) entered into on or after June 21, 1988, and b) fails to meet the 7-pay test; or 2) is received in exchange for a contract that meets the requirements of 1).

Internal Revenue Service (IRS) - The U.S. government agency responsible for the collection and enforcement of taxes, primarily income and employment taxes, but also corporate, gift, excise and estate taxes.

Last In, First Out (LIFO) - A method of managing and determining the value of assets that assumes an entity sells, uses or disposes of its most recently acquired funds first. If an asset is sold for less than it is acquired for, then the difference is considered a capital loss. If an asset is sold for more than it is acquired for, the difference is considered a capital gain. This can be a tax advantage or liability.

LIFO - (see **Last In, First Out**)

liquidity - The ability to convert an asset to cash.

Long Term Care insurance (LTC) - Insurance that provides for care in the form of home-health care, nursing-home care, personal or adult day care for an individual age 65 or older that has a chronic or disabling health condition or needs constant supervision.

longevity insurance protection (LIP) – LIP is a term created by the Author. It refers to an income rider on an annuity contract designed to pay to the insured a benefit for life, no matter how long the annuitant lives. When the annuitant dies, the spouse may continue the benefit for life provided 'joint' pay-out was elected.

lost decade - Refers to the time period between 1991 and 2001 when economic growth in Japan was at a standstill. The Author also uses this term to describe the market volatility in the U.S. from

2000-2010 because pension plans and other investments experience losses that offset gains such that a majority of the Equity Market investors saw similar account balances in 1999, 2007 and 2011.

LTC - (see **Long Term Care insurance**)

market volatility - The amount of uncertainty concerning the changes in a security's value. A higher volatility means that the price of the security can change dramatically over a short time period in either direction. A lower volatility means that a security's value does not fluctuate dramatically, but changes in value at a steady pace over a period of time.

maturity date - The date at which the principal amount of a life insurance policy becomes payable, either by death or other contract stipulation.

MEC (see **Modified Endowment Contract**)

modified endowment contract (**MEC**) - A life insurance policy in which the cumulative premium payments exceed certain amounts specified under the Internal Revenue Code 72 (e) to enable tax-free withdrawals or loans. As in any life insurance policy, the death benefit payable to the beneficiary is not subject to income tax.

money market account - A financial account that pays interest based on current interest rates in the money markets (financial institutions and dealers in money or credit who wish to either borrow or lend).

monthly point to Point - A fixed index annuity indexing method that calculates the percentage change between prices of a specified stock market index on each of the monthly anniversary dates, applies a specified cap rate to determine the monthly capped percentage changes, and adds the monthly capped percentages changes to determine the annual interest amount that is credited to a particular fixed index annuity contract each contract year.

mutual fund - An investment vehicle comprised of a pool of funds collected from many investors so that the money can be invested in securities like stocks, bonds, money market accounts, etc.

NASDAQ 100 - The stock market index of 100 of the largest non-financial companies, both U.S. and outside the U.S.

opt out - A type of 401(k) plan that allows the employee to change the terms of an employee sponsored plan, or opt out of it completely if they do not want to participate.

Permanent life insurance - A type of life insurance policy that does not expire and combines a death benefit with a savings portion.

POM POM – acronym meaning Peace of Mind and Plenty of Money.

Ponzi Scheme - A fraudulent investment operation that pays returns to its investors from their own money or the money paid by other investors, rather than from profit earned by the individual or organization running the operation.

portfolio - The term used to refer to the various securities a person is investing in. Otherwise known as investment portfolio.

premium - The amount of money invested in an insurance policy.

fixed premium - Amount of the payment does not change.

flexible premium - Amount and frequency of payment can change.

single premium - A lump sum of cash is paid into the insurance policy up front so that payment is guaranteed to beneficiaries.

principal - The original amount invested in an insurance policy, original amount of a loan, or face value of a bond.

principal guarantee – A provision in an insurance product that guarantees against losses should the Market index to which the annuity or insurance policy is linked declines in a given year, measured on the anniversary date of the product. The principal in the account would remain at its highest level, unchanged, until the Market index shows increases on another anniversary date, at which time gains are locked in.

principal protection - The guarantee of a fixed-income security than ensures a minimum return equal to the investor's initial investment, or principal.

puts - A form of stock option. Puts increase in value when the security is going down, and decrease in value when the price of the security goes up. A put option allows an individual to sell stock to the investor it was purchased from at a specific price on or before a specific date. See calls.

qualified plan - An investment plan that meets requirements of the Internal Revenue Code and as a result, is eligible to receive certain tax benefits. These plans must be for the exclusive benefit of employees or their beneficiaries. Examples are IRAs, 401(k)s, 457 Plans, TSP , 403(b)s.

RAFT Strategy – An acronym for Retirement Approach Free of Tax, which refers a method of funding and accessing tax-free distributions from an equity indexed universal life insurance policy, designed according to IRS guidelines.

rate of return (ROR) - The gain or loss on an investment over a specified period, expressed as a percentage increase over the initial investment cost.

Raymond James - Raymond James Financial is a diversified holding company providing financial services to individuals, corporations and municipalities through its subsidiary companies that engage primarily in investment.

Required Minimum Distributions (RMD) - the minimum amount that must be withdraw each year from a qualified retirement plan to avoid a penalty, beginning at age 70-1/2 or in the year of retirement.

RMD - (see **Required Minimum Distributions**)

Roaring 20s - A reference to the 1920s, characterizing the decade's distinctive culture in New York City, Paris, London and many other major cities during a period of economic prosperity.

ROR - (see **rate of return**)

Roth IRA – A qualified retirement plan that is funded with after-tax, IRS-specified, limited contributions and enjoys tax-free growth, distributions and transfer to beneficiaries. Unlike a traditional IRA, contributions may be made to a Roth IRA after age 70 ½.

Rule of 72 - A rule stating that in order to find the number of years required to double your money at a given interest rate, you divide the compound return into 72. The result is the approximate number of years that it will take for your investment to double.

Rule of 100 - A financial rule in which an investor subtracts his age from 100 and the resultant sum suggests the maximum amount of one's portfolio that should be exposed to risk.

S&P 500 - Standard & Poor's 500 is a stock market index based on the market capitalizations of 500 leading companies publicly traded in the U.S. stock market.

Section 1035 Exchange - A tax-free exchange of an existing annuity contract for a new one; typically by closing the annuity contract with one insurance company and opening a new contract with another company using the same money.

September 11th, 2001 - The day a series of four terrorist attacks coordinated by the Islamic terrorist group al-Qaeda were carried out in the Washington, D.C. area and New York City. The attacks had a significant economic impact on the U.S. and world markets.

simple interest - A quick method of calculating the interest charge on a loan. Simple interest is determined by multiplying the interest rate by the principal by the number of periods. It does not compound with the account.

Social Security – Is a comprehensive Federal government program that provides eligible individuals with income. Eligibility is determined by age, circumstance, and the amount one has contributed to the system i.e., disabled individuals, children who have lost a parent, retirees and their dependents. It has historically been financed by assessment of employers and employees.

stock market - A public entity used to trade company stocks and derivatives at an agreed price; also known as equity market. Examples are the New York Stock Exchange (NYSE), Toronto Stock Exchange, Tokyo Stock Exchange and so forth.

stocks - The equity the owners of an incorporated business have in that business. Stock is divided into shares and represents a fraction of ownership in a business.

Strategic Roll-Out – A term used by the Author to explain a method of taking money from an IRA, paying the tax and contributing the balance to the RAFT Strategy in an effort to build a tax-free retirement nest egg.

Strategic Wealth Coach (SWC) - A financial specialist, trained and licensed in the State(s) in which he or she does business. An SWC provides financial and retirement planning, especially using the Triple Crown Solution.

stretch IRA - An estate planning concept that extends the financial life of an IRA across multiple generations. The IRA can be passed from generation to generation and allows the beneficiaries to enjoy tax-deferred and/or tax-free growth for as long as possible.

surrender period - The period of time one must wait before taking money out of an annuity without penalty.

surrender value - The amount of money and insurance company will pay to the policy holder or annuity holder when that holder voluntarily terminates the policy before its maturity or the insured event occurs.

SWC - (see **Strategic Wealth Coach**)

T-bill - Treasury bill, which is a short-term debt obligation backed by the U.S. government with a maturity date of less than one year.

TAMRA (see **Technical and Miscellaneous Revenue Act of 1988**)

tax bracket - The rate at which an individual is taxed, based on one's income level.

tax-deferred - Investment earnings that accumulate and compound tax-free until the investor withdraws and takes possession of them, at which time, the owner is assessed regular income tax by the IRS. The most common types of tax-deferred investments include those in individual retirement accounts (IRAs) and tax-deferred annuities.

Tax Equity and Fiscal Responsibility Act of 1982 (**TEFRA**) - A U.S. Federal law that took away some of the effects of the Kemp-Roth Act of 1981. With the passage of the TEFRA, Congress provided a mechanism to allow distributions from a permanent life insurance policy to be accessed tax-free.

tax favored - An investment that does not tax its profits as much as other types of investments.

tax-free - A financial product that is not assessed State or Federal tax.

tax shelter - A legal method of reducing one's taxable income. The most common type of tax shelter is an employer-sponsored 401(k) plan.

Tech Bubble - The positive outlook by investors towards high tech companies on the stock market that existed between 1995 and 2002. As a Tech Bubble is forming, investors collectively believed special opportunities existed in the stock market, resulting in the purchase of stocks at a price higher than they would normally consider.

Technical and Miscellaneous Revenue Act of 1988 (**TAMRA**) – For insurance purposes, TAMRA created a new category of life insurance policy called a Modified Endowment Contract (MEC). TAMRA defines such a contract as one which fails to meet certain premium limitation tests, first on an annual and then on a cumulative basis. The TAMRA test period runs for 7 years from the time it starts, hence its common name, the "7-Pay Test".

TEFRA (see **Tax Equity and Fiscal Responsibility Act of 1982**)

term life insurance policy - Life insurance that covers a limited period of time and has a fixed rate of payments.

Thrift Savings Plan (TSP) - A retirement savings and investment plan for Federal employees and members of the uniformed services, including the Ready Reserve. It offers the same types of savings and tax benefits that many private corporations offer their employees under 401(k) plans.

TSP - (see **Thrift Savings Plan**)

UL (see **universal life insurance**)

Uncle Sam - A common personification of the U.S. government.

universal life insurance (UL) - A type of flexible permanent life insurance that offers the low-cost of term life along with a savings element, similar to whole life insurance, that is invested to provide a higher cash value.

variable universal life insurance (VUL) - A type of permanent life insurance policy that builds cash value amd is typically invested in mutual funds and/or individual stocks. The cash value fluctuates according to its earnings and is subject to risk.

venture capital - The financing given to early-stage, high potential, high risk start-up companies.

VUL (see **variable universal life insurance**)

wash loan -A tax-free loan taken out on an insurance policy; also known as Zero spread loan.

whole life insurance policy - A life insurance contract that has both an insurance and an investment component. The insurance component pays a stated amount upon death of the insured. The investment component accumulates a cash value that the policyholder can withdraw or borrow against.

Y2K - The transition of technical data at the onset of the year 2000. caused by the programing of computer software and hardware not recognizing the Year 2000 accurately. Y2K has had effects on the economy prior to and after the year 2000.

zero spread loan - (see **wash loan**)

Resources

72 (t) 72 (q) www.IRS.gov:
http://www.irs.gov/irb/2007-05_IRB/ar11.html

Bloomberg:
http://www.bloomberg.com/news/2012-08-15/cost-of-college-degree

Bureau of Labor and Statistics:
http://www.bls.gov/data/inflation_calculator.htm

Consumer Price Index Calculator:
http://www.usinflationcalculator.com/inflation/consumer-price-index-and-annual-percent-changes-from-1913-to-2008/

Historical CD rates:
http://www.bankrate.com/finance/cd/current-interest-rates.aspx

Investopedia:
http://www.investopedia.com/terms/e/equity-indexed-universal-life-insurance.asp
http://www.investopedia.com/terms/s/stockmarket.asp

TEFRA, DEFRA, TAMRA www.IRS.gov:
http://www.irs.gov/irb/2008-35_IRB/ar10.html

Roth IRA Guidelines:
http://www.trustetc.com/equity-university/irs-contribution-limits.html

State Guarantee Fund:
http://www.annuityadvantage.com/stateguarantee.htm

Stretch IRA and 72(t) Calculators:
http://www.dinkytown.net/java/StretchIRA.html
http://www.dinkytown.net/java/Retire72T.html

Tax Code Definitions:
http://www.law.cornell.edu/uscode

Wikipedia:
http://en.wikipedia.org/wiki/Universal_life_insurance
http://en.wikipedia.org/wiki/Indexed_life
http://en.wikipedia.org/wiki/Variable_universal_life_insurance

About the Cover

D id you ever wake up in the middle of the night with an image in your head that seems to be the solution to your challenge? That is exactly what happened to me just over a year ago while I was considering what image would I place on the _RAFT Strategy_ book cover.

Because of the business I engage in every day, I often go to bed with numbers swimming around in my head; numbers that are continually attacked by the rushing waters of inflation, the turbulence of stock market volatility and the floods of increasing taxes. What better way to protect a precious Golden Nest Egg against these financial tsunamis than in the safety of a seaworthy LifeRAFT?

When I think of the retirement challenges many of us face every day and in the future, I picture a Nest Egg safely bobbing along in my Tax-Free LifeRAFT, basking in the warm sunshine of Principal Protection.

It didn't take me long to convey to my son Pace the vision of this powerful, yet serene picture. He gathered the elements and created our signature book cover.

My hope is that every reader can take comfort in knowing that the LifeRAFT is there to preserve, protect, and perpetuate their nest egg. All they need to do is learn how to launch it.

CPSIA information can be obtained at www.ICGtesting.com
Printed in the USA
BVOW08s0907250713

326857BV00003B/4/P

9 781626 976993